A WAY THROUGH THE OLD TESTAMENT
1.

JOSEPH RHYMER

The Beginnings of a People

A way through the
Old Testament

1. The Pentateuch

Chart and Maps
designed and executed by Paul Colsell
to the author's specifications

SHEED AND WARD
LONDON AND MELBOURNE

FIRST PUBLISHED 1967
SHEED AND WARD LTD
33 MAIDEN LANE
LONDON W.C.2
AND
SHEED AND WARD PTY LTD
28 BOURKE STREET
MELBOURNE

NIHIL OBSTAT: JOANNES M. T. BARTON, S.T.D., C.S.S.
   CENSOR DEPUTATUS

IMPRIMATUR ✠ PATRITIUS CASEY, VIC. GEN.

WESTMONASTERII, DIE 5A OCTOBRIS 1966

The *Nihil obstat* and *Imprimatur* are a declaration that a
book is considered to be free from doctrinal or moral error.
It is not implied that those who have granted the *Nihil obstat*
and *Imprimatur* agree with the contents, opinions, or statements expressed.

This book is set in 11 pt. Linotype Times

Made and printed in Great Britain by
William Clowes and Sons, Limited, London and Beccles

To Ann and Derek Henderson

Contents

Preface

More than three thousand years ago, early in the year and at the time of the full moon, a group of people fled by night from their villages in Egypt and made for the desert. They were foreign settlers forcibly employed by the Egyptians in the building of government granaries; against every expectation, they succeeded in getting away.

Their experience that night, and in the days that followed, left its mark on them for ever. It made them into a nation and it released a force whose effects have been felt throughout the world. It made them the Jews. In that experience the Jewish people discovered the heart of their religion, the power at work in every detail of their daily lives and their national history. From that experience they have drawn the strength to emerge from overwhelming disaster with their faith unshaken, whether the oppressor has worn a Babylonian breastplate or an SS jackboot, for during that Egyptian night they found God.

The word they used to express this experience of God present and active amongst them was 'covenant'. 'God has made a covenant with his people'. By this they meant that he had promised them the security of a land of their own, and that they would become a great nation; but above all they had received the promise of his presence and protection. And on their part they had to become the kind of people God wanted them to be: reflections of his power and examples of his love. For they were to be the centre from which God could conquer his world again and restore his creation to the perfection for which he had made it. They knew themselves to be the intimate friends of God, and with this privilege they received an equally great responsibility. It took them very many generations to explore the full consequences and meaning of it all, but the heart of the matter was there at the beginning when God brought them out of Egypt and made them the people of the covenant.

Any national movement of this magnitude is worth exploring, but we have further reasons for doing so. For we, too, are the people of a covenant, and, like the ancient Jews, our covenant is also grounded on an event in history and confirmed with promises. Our covenant rests on the birth, death and resurrection of Jesus Christ, and with it go his promises that he will be with us until the end of the world, pouring God's power and love into all who wish to become part of his people. And we, too, have responsibilities as great as our privileges, the responsibility of becoming more and more like the God who pours his love into us, and of extending the power of that love throughout his world.

There is even more to it than that, for it is the same God who has made the covenants. The privileges and responsibilities of the new covenant are continuous with those of the old, extensions of the intimacy which began on that Egyptian night and which reached its climax in the upper room when God's son said, 'This is my body ... This is my blood ... of the new covenant.' Here there is mystery deeper than anything else we can experience, mystery which opens and expands limitlessly as we explore it. As we set out to discover the wonders of our own new covenant, the events of the old covenant and the experiences of the people who were involved in it are an enormous help to us.

What should our approach be? More than anything else, we must at all costs avoid an attitude of superiority. For the people of the old covenant, God was the heart of their lives and the key to their everyday actions. If we merely see their religion as an inadequate foreshadowing of Christianity we shall fail from the beginning. Their experience must be explored with the deepest sympathy if we are to understand it and benefit from it; we must feel with their feelings, see their world through their eyes, and know their longing for God.

It was an effective religion, an experience which could produce sanctity of the highest order; it was the faith of the girl whose reply to God has become the pattern of all faith:

And Mary said, Behold, I am the handmaid of the Lord; let it be to me according to your word.

JOSEPH RHYMER

Kersham, Christmas 1966

Introduction: the information

This book is about the beginnings of a people: their emergence out of obscurity, the ordeal and experience which turned them from an insignificant and oppressed minority into a nation, and their first experiments in living with the God who had chosen them and made them what they were. The beginnings of most nations are obscure and difficult to study with any confidence or accuracy. Usually even the material for study is scarce, for before they become important and powerful there is little incentive for people to record and preserve the details of their insignificant lives, and even the technique and materials for writing may be lacking. Where there are records it is all too likely that they may have been coloured and rewritten to reflect the interests of later editors, for every historian approaches his materials, the information at his disposal, with some particular point of view or with questions he is trying to answer. The use he makes of his materials, the parts he selects for mention and comment, will depend on the view he takes, the problem he is trying to illuminate, or even on the teaching he is trying to support. At its worst all this produces partisan propaganda, but even at its very best it means that the reader will be seeing the view through someone else's eyes. This problem is particularly acute when we try to find what happened when the ancient Hebrews, the people of the Old Testament, first emerged as a nation.

The early history of the Jews is a complicated subject for several reasons. For one thing, the distance separating us in time is so large. The people claimed that the beginnings of their story must be sought in the time of Abraham, who probably lived about 1800 BC, nearly four thousand years away from our own times. It is doubtful if there was anyone amongst the Hebrews who could write at that time, and even four hundred years later, at the time of the exodus when the people escaped from Egypt, writing seems to have played very little part in their lives. For us, who live in such a state of dependence on the written word, this is a situation almost impossible to imagine. How can we have any knowledge of those times, and how can we trust such information as is available? At least part of the answer to this is to see just how the knowledge has come down to us, and examine how reliable the methods were.

At first the nation's early traditions were passed on down the generations and across the various divisions of the people by word of mouth; we are tempted to compare this with the notori-

ous inaccuracy of rumour, but in fact the old oral
tradition was far more accurate than we easily
realise. The stories of earlier times were told
again and again at the local sanctuaries, the district centres of sacrifice, whenever the people
gathered for the regular feasts. Not only the
story-tellers, but many of the audience as well
would know every word and detail of the stories
by heart—the result of constant repetition and
of memories honed razor sharp—for when the
majority of people cannot read or write an accurate memory becomes outstandingly important. Any deviation from the authentic tradition
would have excited immediate comment, and
when the stories were about God's activity
amongst his chosen people reverence would rein-
force memory. Any alteration would certainly
have been resisted.

Yet we can be equally certain that there was
alteration, or at least expansion and development of the tradition to meet the needs of the
story-teller and his audience, and this is the
second great difficulty a modern reader finds as
he explores the accounts these people left of their
history. Nowadays we have come to accept and
take for granted certain standards about historical writing. We expect it to be dispassionate, un-
biassed, and that it will present a balanced view
of the period it is showing to us. The ancient
Hebrews had none of these concerns. They were
only anxious to show God present and active in
their nation's history and making his presence
felt again and again as they called on him in their

3

need. By this criterion alone they judged the value of a document or of a memory, and they were even prepared to alter and select if it served this purpose. Only one thing mattered: God had chosen them and made them a people, and he would defend them against anyone, no matter how powerful, who tried to prevent him from working his will through them. At first sight this is alarming, for it offends our reverence for historical truth, but it is worth noticing that at least this approach points to the great power of the belief which could so draw on the whole range of experience and use it for its own purposes. God was certainly no mere remote principle or impersonal force belonging to an earlier age: he was present in their midst, and the age-old methods by which he worked could be seen in the events of their own day.

Whatever it was that happened early in their history to produce such a belief, it was an event which left the deepest of impressions on those who experienced it, and this impression they successfully transmitted to the people who came after them. It is this experience that we are going to examine. Our main sources will be the first five books of the Old Testament, Genesis to Deuteronomy, for they are almost entirely concerned with it. As we examine what these books have to say it is worth bearing in mind the effect such an incident as D-Day has had on our memories of the last war. Events which we now see were leading up to D-Day and people who played a prominent part in it are selected for comment and given a prominence which was often far from evident at the time. Now that we can see the whole pattern of the war we can organise our memories and understand and control the available material. So too with the exodus; by it the experiences of a vital period in the history of a people were controlled and organised so that they could be understood.

The exodus dominated Hebrew history to a far greater extent than any of the events which have affected our own times, and we shall never understand the Hebrews' account of their history if we do not bear this in mind. It was the 'fact for faith', the event by which they explained everything which had happened to their people both before and after it. Every act of the people who lived before it, every detail of their lives, helped to create the situation in Egypt; everything that happened afterwards found its explanation and cause in the great escape when God brought his people out with a high hand and an outstretched arm. The whole of this people's historical writing can be seen as a commentary on the exodus: a constantly deepening exploration of the experience which found its centre in the crossing of the Red Sea, the defeat of the Egyptian army and the awareness of the power of God active amongst them. Each new crisis and period in the nation's life for more than a thousand years, whether of disaster or of triumph, was used to cast new light on the exodus and deepen their understanding of their God's power and of the relationship he established with them. There he had chosen them, and their exploration of the ancient event—their constant meditation on it in the light of their own contemporary experience—is the key to the understanding of their writings and of the contradictions to be found there. This is particularly true of the main sources we must use, Genesis to Deuteronomy. Very little of the contents of these early books of the Old Testament actually dates from the time of the exodus, and certainly no longer can anyone seriously think that they were written by Moses. He is indeed the dominant figure in them, and this is a fact of great importance to which we shall be returning, but it is no more than an ancient pious fiction that he himself wrote them. Their origins and evolution until they reached the form in which we now know them was a complicated process spanning hundreds of years and showing the influence of a great deal of Hebrew history, and because these books are our main sources it is essential that we look at something of this process which brought them to birth.

The early history of the people, and particularly the great experience of the escape from Egypt, was first preserved not in writing but in the spoken word, the stories passed on from father to son and from priest to congregation. This oral tradition varied in detail from sanctuary to sanctuary and from district to district. As sections of the people developed their own local customs, so too they would concentrate on particular sections of the tradition and give them prominence, particularly if they thought they were connected with someone who had played an important part in the events the tradition preserved. A family which traced its descent from Aaron would naturally highlight the part he played, the priests of Shechem would draw attention to the incidents which the tradition located there—and if there were points where the tradition failed to give a location they would no doubt be ready to provide the hospitality of their own sanctuary. The tradition covered a wide field, for although the Jews called these first five books 'The Law', they deal with matters far wider than law in the sense in which we use the word. Law there was, but there was also history, poetry, customs covering the whole range of national life, and the religious events and practices which so penetrated the people's existence. Some of the more important parts of the tradition, particularly some of the legal matters, were cast in forms specially designed for memorising so that everyone present in court—and with cases heard at the village gate this might be every able man—could tell if the law was being correctly applied. Clearly, in a situation like this, the preservation of the traditions had a high priority, and this may account for the importance attached to the hereditary character of the priesthood. Part of the priest's job was to guard the purity of the tradition, to see that the people knew it, and to make sure that it was handed on safely and accurately. Malachi laid great store by this when he set out the responsibilities of the priesthood:

> True instruction was in his mouth, and no
> wrong was found on his lips. He walked with
> me in peace and uprightness, and he turned
> many from iniquity. For the lips of a priest
> should guard knowledge, and men should seek
> instruction from his mouth, for he is the mes-
> senger of the Lord of hosts. [Mal 2:6–7]

and he went on to condemn his contemporaries
for failing in this.

For nearly two hundred and fifty years after
the exodus the main strands of tradition grew
and developed. When people of different districts
came into contact with each other—through marriage, or when an army was raised—the strands
of tradition crossed, mingled and separated
again, carrying with them borrowed fragments.
For all that, there were local variations; there
were also control and consistency so that the main
pattern remained accurate. Fortunately, after
about two hundred and fifty years, the people
were united, probably for the first time in their
history, under the dynamic rule of the greatest
king they ever had, David. Until his reign they
had been at least distinct groups of people, separated by a broad belt of land running across the
middle of the country which remained firmly
in the hands of the original inhabitants. The
Hebrew people had penetrated into Palestine in
two distinct groups, one from the south and the
other across the Jordan just north of the Dead
Sea, and it is very probable that only one of these
groups—the northern one—had been in Egypt.

The occupation of the country seems to have been more a process of infiltration than of conquest, and stretched over many years. David completed the process by capturing a key position in the central belt and making it his capital, Jerusalem, and from that day on the nation had a centre which has held their loyalty until the present day. Their new-found unity was not to last long; in fact it only just survived the reign of David's son Solomon, but it was long enough for the tradition to be stabilised and fixed before it could disintegrate into unreliable folk-legend.

Solomon died, and his son, too weak to control the forces his father had ruled, saw the kingdom split again into two warring factions—a split never to be healed until the northern group, the kingdom of Israel, were annihilated by the terrifying ruthlessness of Assyria two hundred years later. With this split the tradition again began to develop along separate paths, but soon the growing use of writing was to fix the two main strands in forms which we can still trace today. There was still nothing we would recognise as the bible we now know, but at least there was something later editors could draw on when they were re-telling the nation's history and showing how the hand of God was to be seen at work in every stage of it. The first of these editors, the great line of anonymous scribes and priests who wrote the bulk of the Old Testament, worked about 720 BC when the northern kingdom fell. He saved the northern part of the tradition and wove it with the southern to give a movingly vivid and simple account of the people's origins, from the creation of the world until the escape from Egypt and the occupation of the land in which they lived. The second account of the creation of the world, the one that starts in the middle of Gn 2:4, is his work:

> ... then the Lord God formed man of dust from the ground, and breathed into his nostrils the breath of life; and man became a living being. And the Lord God planted a garden in Eden, in the east; and there he put the man whom he had formed ... [Gn 2:7f]

Just before him, and perhaps inspiring his work, came the first two of the prophets whose writings and teachings have come down to us, Amos and Hosea. Both were intimately involved in the attempts to save the northern kingdom from the disaster looming over it, and although they seem to have failed it is possible that the saving of the tradition, and the realisation that the exodus lies at the heart of the Hebrew faith, is their true achievement.

Less conspicuous, but soon to become outstandingly important, was another kind of tradition intimately woven into the national life at all levels: the law. Like our law, it covered the whole range of activity, from the inner intimacy of the family, through the villages' agricultural economy and the towns' merchant life, to the needs which affected the whole nation—the kingship and the central worship in Jerusalem, or the organisation of war. It recognised and controlled every kind of person: king, slave, wife, child, stranger, orphan, widow, and it drew its wisdom from the accumulated experience of centuries of legal decision. Some of the law was taken from surrounding nations, some the people brought with them from their nomad life in the desert; they took over the laws (especially those relating to agriculture) of the people already in the land when they entered it, and they learned law as their elders tried cases in the publicity of the open space around the village gate. By the early years of the seventh century BC there was a considerable body of law; parts of it are quoted unaltered in the Book of Exodus and elsewhere, and we can tell from the variations in language that there had been little attempt to revise or codify it. More important, the law seems to have been largely secular at this stage, and the need to explain why the law should be kept was not felt; the empirical needs of the community and the punishments which followed breaches of the law were thought to be sufficient. Sufficient, that is, until the reign of Manasseh brought degradation and vice to an extent no earlier king had attempted. The smoke of the sacrificial fires outside the south wall of Jerusalem, where children were burned alive to Moloch, was the sign that the law had to be strengthened—and strengthened in a way which could bring even a king back to the purpose God had for this people.

Someone, or some group, probably in Jerusalem, codified the law and wrote into it the spirit of the exodus, the memory of the moment when the power of their God was unmistakably active and the people were saved from the obscurity and slavery of Egypt. They rewrote the law in the way they thought Moses would have written it if he had been alive in their times, and the result is the greater part of what we now call Deuteronomy, the fifth book of the bible. It was probably the first of the biblical books to appear in anything like the form we now know them, for although later editors added to it, particularly by expanding the introduction and conclusion, the great central sections of law, chapters 12 to 26, are the work of the original authors. It does not really concern us here that the reform based on Deuteronomy—despite its initial spectacular success—finally failed. What does matter is to see the background for this particular account of the exodus: a revision of the law, in the face of desperate national need, six hundred years after the event. Deuteronomy may have a great deal to tell us about seventh-century Judah, and about the fatal years which ended so dramatically when the Babylonians destroyed Jerusalem and swept the people into a new slavery, but only with the greatest caution can we use the book as evidence about the exodus.

Parallel with the country's legal institutions, and as important in the nation's life, was another institution with a complex and traditional organisation: the religious structure based on a chain of sacrificial centres, the local sanctuaries with their officiating priests. As we have seen, the priests had a particular responsibility for the preservation of the tradition, quite apart from their sacrificial duties, and this was helped by the hereditary character of the priesthood. While the sanctuaries existed, and particularly the central sanctuary, the temple in Jerusalem, there was little need for written instructions. The regular round of sacrifices, from the daily ones to the great harvest festivals, would be performed and supervised by priests many of whom had taken part in them again and again. The corporate memory and experience of the professional priests would suffice as long as they were grouped round a sacrificing centre nourishing a living tradition. But in 587 BC both Jerusalem and the temple were reduced to heaps of uninhabitable ruins, and the bulk of the people —certainly any with an official position or with any trace of education—were deported to Babylon. With the destruction of the temple and the fading of the hopes of any speedy return to Jerusalem, it became vital to make sure that the temple traditions were not lost as the older priests died off in exile. The traditions were no longer safe in the hands of young priests who had possibly never taken part in a sacrifice.

The priests in exile began to set down the ritual of the temple and, indeed, everything they thought might be needed when it became possible to build it again. Ezekiel was the first, so far as we know, to realise this need, just as he was the first to realise that the exile in Babylon was going to be a long business, and his blueprint for the restored temple is given at the end of his prophecies, chapters 40 to 48 of Ezekiel. The priests were confident that even if several generations had to pass before the people could return to their native land God would not desert them or allow their enemies to remain unpunished. Some of the psalms probably belong to this period, not just the songs of anger and despair, but such poems as this (Ps. 126):

When the Lord restored the fortunes of Zion,
　　we were like those who dream.
Then our mouth was filled with laughter,
　　and our tongue with shouts of joy;
Then they said among the nations,
　　The Lord has done great things for them.
The Lord has done great things for us;
　　We are glad.
Restore our fortunes, O Lord,
　　Like the water-courses in the Negeb!
May those who sow in tears
　　reap with shouts of joy!
He that goes forth weeping,
　　bearing the seed for sowing,
Shall come home with shouts of joy,
　　bringing his sheaves with him.

The sudden filling of the dry desert water-courses with the rushing spate of a cloudburst was an apt image for their hope in God's faithfulness and swift power.

The priests recorded the dimensions of the temple, the vestments of the priests and all the details of the ritual of worship. And because it was essential that all this should be given the authority of God—for it was all the expression of the covenant he had made with the people, and of the constant renewal of that covenant through the sacrifices—the priests set the whole body of regulations within the period when the covenant was established. Like the lawyers before them, the priests recorded their customs and regulations and traditions as if it was all established in its full complexity during the journeying in the wilderness immediately after the escape from Egypt, for this was when the covenant had been made. The first five books of the bible were beginning to take the form in which we now know them: the exodus story and, interwoven with it, the accumulated law and ritual which had developed during the following eight centuries. This process may be seen at work almost everywhere one dips into the second half of Exodus, or in Leviticus and Numbers:

> Then the Lord said to Aaron, And behold, I have given you whatever is kept of the offerings made to me, all the consecrated things of the people of Israel; I have given them to you as a portion, and to your sons as a perpetual due ... All the best of the oil, and all the best of the wine and of the grain, the first fruits of what they give to the Lord, I give to you ... [Nm 18:8–12]

Or again:

> The Lord said to Moses, This shall be the law of the leper for the day of his cleansing. He

15

shall be brought to the priest; and the priest shall go out of the camp, and the priest shall make an examination. Then if the leprous disease is healed in the leper, the priest shall command them to take for him who is to be cleansed two living clean birds and cedarwood and scarlet stuff and hyssop; and the priest shall command them to kill one of the birds in an earthen vessel over running water ... [Lv 14:1ff]

and so on through all the detailed ritual of rehabilitating those whose contagious condition had constituted a danger to the community. Here again we must be very careful before we accept all this as a description of the exodus situation.

Recording ritual and priestly privileges was not the only concern of the exiled priests, nor their main achievement. The shock of devastation and exile provoked the deepest theological reflection on the workings of God and the place of the nation in the divine scheme. This thinking reached its highest level in the writings of the Second Isaiah, the anonymous prophet of the later part of the exile whose work is to be found from chapter forty onwards in the Book of the Prophet Isaiah. He took the insights of his predecessors to their sublime conclusions and gave the captive Hebrews a vision of God omnipotent, omnipresent, and omniscient, in control of every detail of history and using all nations for the achievement of his purposes. This prophet's writings will be examined in a later book; our concern here is to notice the influence he had on the priests in exile, for they took his vision of God and worked out the implications of it in detail throughout the history of the world. Looking back down their national history, they showed God's hand at work in it from the very creation of the world. The magnificent opening of Genesis, with its sweeping prospect of a world utterly dependent on the continually outpoured creative power of God, with man as God's viceroy set as a focus of unity and order at the centre of creation, all this is the work of the priests in exile. At the centre of that activity, the goal towards which it all moved and the spring from which the subsequent history of the people flowed, they set the exodus, and they saw the whole history of the world as a pattern of selection and choice, by their omnipotent God, of instruments through which he could work his will and draw the whole creation into his love.

The priests took the nation's traditions, the folk-tales and the sacred history, and they arranged them within an explanatory framework in order to show how all the events fitted into one great scheme of salvation. Reading it in this light, it is easy to see how the belief in a coming messiah and in the restoration of the nation's glory gained such force in the years following the exile. Above all the priests taught that without God man is utterly helpless, unable to obtain food or find safety, and even unable to govern himself: everything is from God, and if men turn away from God they only bring upon themselves misery, disunity, and destruction. The covenant with God was not to be seen merely as a desirable thing, a convenience conferring prosperity and privilege: it was vital for life itself and for everything that made life possible. This truth was the fruit which grew from the bitter experience of the exile in Babylon, and the priests were determined that it should be seen reflected in every detail of their people's history.

Genesis to Deuteronomy (the first five books of the Old Testament) are the lasting monument of the priests' great achievement, and they did their job effectively. The people went into exile a nation, but they returned from it a church— and a church so conscious of their identity that the members gave it their first loyalty no matter where they happened to live. Indeed, so strong was their sense of having a special covenant with God that it produced the exclusiveness and impression of superiority which have so often been their comfort in persecution. In its acute form this national pride stood in the way of the recognition of Jesus Christ:

> Jesus then said to the Jews who had believed in him, If you continue in my word, you are truly my disciples, and you will know the truth, and the truth will make you free. They answered him, We are descendants of Abraham, and have never been in bondage to anyone. How is it that you say, You will be made free? [Jn 8:31–33]

The glory and tragedy of later Jewish history is not our concern here. We are concerned with the beginnings, the early history, but it has been essential to look at some of the later history because it has so radically affected the information we have about the earlier. We must use this information because there is nothing else—but also because the very extent to which those early events have been made the explanation of everything which happened afterwards shows how great an effect those events had on the people who took part in them. We shall be safe enough if we try to bear in mind that we are seeing it all through the eyes of people with very different problems from ours: people exiled into slavery, or faced with a country riddled with the foulest distortions of religion, or even only concerned that the nation was split into two sections jealous of each other and manoeuvring for power.

Although we shall be concentrating on events which occurred towards the end of the thirteenth century BC: the escape from Egypt, the crossing of the Red Sea, and the experience in the wilderness which confirmed the people's belief that God had entered into a special covenant with them, it will be essential to set these central events in their context. That context begins with the emergence of Abraham, about 1800 BC, continues with the events which took the Hebrews into Egypt and concludes, after the exodus itself, with the penetration of the Hebrews into Palestine and their early difficulties there. All this forms a convenient historical period, for their history took a new turn when they moved away from the old casual form of government by which each new emergency produced a leader to deal with it. About the year 1050 BC they elected a king, and although in many ways King Saul has a foot in both kinds of government, he clearly marks the start of a new era and it will be convenient to stop at the end of the 'judges' who came before him.

The period we shall be examining is of vital importance for ourselves, for it contains one of the most influential religious experiences in history, an experience as influential for Judaism as the cross and resurrection are for Christianity—indeed it is no exaggeration to say that the exodus is the main key to the understanding of the New Testament experience. But if we are to gain access to it we must first forget our own times and needs, and concentrate our attention on the people to whom the experience came. In particular we shall find ourselves giving special attention to Moses, the man who dominated the whole period, who saw the events through God's eyes and communicated to his people the faith by which it all made sense. It requires that we alter our angle of vision and fix our attention and interest on what was urgent to the ancient Hebrews. Only then, when we have entered their experience, will we see the relevance of their faith to our needs.

Diagrammatic chart showing the development of the Pentateuch

The chart on p. 23 below is intended to provide a visual summary of the information contained in this Introduction, and at the same time to act as a convenient reference for readers to use during their reading of the subsequent chapters of this book.

2—B.O.P.

In the chart opposite, showing the development of the story of the exodus from the early oral traditions to the fully developed first five books of the Old Testament, it has not been possible to show how much the three main lines of development influenced each other. It is important to realise that law, history, and worship did not develop independently of each other. The people who were involved in lawsuits or listened to the cases being heard were the same ones who worshipped in the temple or the local sanctuaries and were inspired by the stories of their nation's history. Nor were the collection and transmission of the various parts of the tradition thought of as the responsibility of different people. Historians and lawyers would all probably be priests. The tradition developed as a unified whole, and the strands of it have only been separated in the chart to help show the external influences on its development. The thick lines are like the strands of a rope which has been unravelled to show how it is constructed. In fact, of course, this is not an accurate picture of the rope, for when it is in use the strands are tightly wound together and support each other. So too with the tradition. The scroll symbol in the chart shows the point at which a strand of tradition was written down or influenced an author.

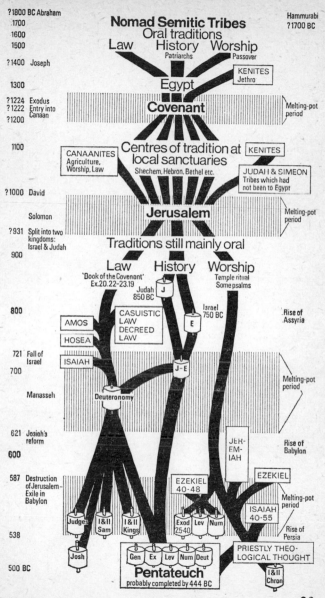

Nomad Semitic Tribes
Oral traditions
Law   History   Worship
Patriarchs   Passover

?1800 BC Abraham	Hammurabi ?1700 BC
1700	
1600	
1500	

?1400 Joseph

1300

KENITES
Jethro

Egypt

?1224 Exodus
?1222 Entry into Canaan
?1200

Covenant

Melting-pot period

1100

CANAANITES
Agriculture, Worship, Law

Centres of tradition at local sanctuaries
Shechem, Hebron, Bethel etc.

KENITES

JUDAH & SIMEON
Tribes which had not been to Egypt

?1000 David

Solomon

Jerusalem

Melting-pot period

?931 Split into two kingdoms: Israel & Judah

900

Traditions still mainly oral

Law   History   Worship
'Book of the Covenant'   Temple ritual
Ex.20.22-23.19   Some psalms

Judah
850 BC   J

800

Israel
750 BC   E

Rise of Assyria

AMOS

HOSEA

CASUISTIC
LAW
DECREED
LAW

721 Fall of Israel

700

ISAIAH

J–E

Melting-pot period

Manasseh

Deuteronomy

621 Josiah's reform

600

JER-EM-IAH

Rise of Babylon

587 Destruction of Jerusalem– Exile in Babylon

EZEKIEL 40-48

EZEKIEL

Melting-pot period

538

Judges   I & II Sam   I & II Kings   Exod 25-40   Lev   Num

ISAIAH 40-55

Rise of Persia

500 BC

Josh   Gen   Ex   Lev   Num   Deut

PRIESTLY THEO-LOGICAL THOUGHT

I & II Chron

Pentateuch
probably completed by 444 BC

23

1

The beginning

> In the beginning God created the heavens and
> the earth. The earth was without form and
> void, and darkness was upon the face of the
> deep; and the Spirit of God was moving over
> the face of the waters. And God said, Let there
> be light; and there was light . . . [Gn 1:1–3]

So the bible begins, and we are given a share in
the faith of a Hebrew priest looking back over
his people's history and seeing there the hand of
God, active and effective. The priest was probably
writing some five centuries before the birth of
Christ, and in Babylon; for the destruction of
Jerusalem and the deportation of the people a
century earlier had stimulated the deepest and
most radical examination into the people's history, a relentless investigation of the causes of the
disaster. From this investigation there had developed a massive theology: a comprehensive and
sweeping conception of the majesty and power
of God and of the place the Hebrew people occupied in his plans. Some of these people had already returned to Jerusalem and begun to build
it again, for the Persians had overthrown the
Babylonians in a great campaign sweeping

across Mesopotamia, and—tolerant beyond
imagination—had sent back home any Jews who
wished to go. With them had gone authority to
rebuild the city, and orders for the local Persian
satrap to finance the rebuilding of the temple and
to endow its services from government funds.
Little wonder that the Second Isaiah, the great
prophet of the later years of the Babylonian cap-
tivity, saw the Persian king as God's tool:

> Thus says the Lord to his anointed, to Cyrus,
>   whose right hand I have grasped,
> to subdue nations before him
>   and ungird the loins of kings,
> to open doors before him
>   that gates may not be closed:
> I will go before you
>   and level the mountains,
> I will break in pieces the doors of bronze
>   and cut asunder the bars of iron,
> I will give you the treasures of darkness
>   and the hoards in secret places,
> That you may know it is I, the Lord, the
>   God of Israel, who call you by your name.
> For the sake of my servant Jacob,
>   and Israel my chosen,
> I call you by your name,
>   I surname you, though you do not know
>   me.
> I am the Lord, and there is no other,
>   besides me there is no God;
>   I gird you, though you do not know me,
> That men may know, from the rising of the
>   sun

and from the west, that there is none be-
   sides me;
I am the Lord, and there is no other.
I form light and create darkness,
   I make peace and create woe,
   I am the Lord, who do all these things.
      [Is 45 : 1–7]

'For the sake of my servant Jacob, and Israel
my chosen . . .' There is the point, the heart of
the priest's view of all history; he assembled and
organised his material to show how it all worked
out, to show the details fitting into their place,
and when he had finished he wrote an introduction which would provide the viewpoint by which
the rest might be understood. That viewpoint
was the vision of God's almighty creative power,
the power which had made the world and everything in it, brought to bear on the Hebrew people.
The same power which had created light, and
seen that it was good, had created the Hebrew
people and seen that they were good, and had
done so in order that the whole creation might
be brought within the sovereign rule of its
creator. This introduction is the first eleven
chapters of the Book of Genesis. The materials
the priest used when he assembled those chapters
were already old, but he selected them to give
the background, the circumstances, of God's call
to Abraham. More than that; like the rest of the
Book of Genesis, their ultimate purpose is to set
the scene for the exodus, the escape from Egypt,
and show that event as the work of the same God

who had made the world. If the conclusion is drawn that he had made the world and called Abraham and the fathers of the nation in order that the exodus from Egypt might take place, then the priestly author would have no objection. Did not the author of Psalm 136 pass without pause straight from the creation of the heavens to the slaughter of the Egyptian first-born? Genesis as a whole is the answer to a 'how' question: 'How did the people come to be in Egypt at all?' But those first introductory chapters are the answer to a 'why' question: 'Why did God exert his power and choose this people and bring them out so dramatically from the humiliation of Egypt?' Because he is the sovereign creator of the whole universe, and it is his will that it be brought back into his steadfast love.

The separation from that love was man's fault alone. That conclusion had been reached long before the disaster of Babylon. The speculation had probably reached its final form about the time of King David's son, Solomon, and been passed on ready for the priestly editor to use. Man had quickly disobeyed the God who had created him, and had found himself exiled from the harmony God had intended for him. Food had now to be grown with sweat, animals had become dangerous, the first murder occurred and there was a beginning to inter-tribal warfare. God returned his creation to the water from which he brought it, saving only one family and representative animals, but the seed of dis-harmony had been sown, and the efforts of

Noah's descendants to climb back to heaven collapsed in the confusion of Babel. It is a convenient explanation of the state of the world, and we must not make more of it than that. It is a description of a situation, the situation which called for the outpouring of God's creative power if his world was to be saved; it is not a textbook of the early history of the world. This is the material the priestly editor used; but in using it he left his mark upon it, for he set it in a framework of divine choice. He showed God's plan working out from the very beginning in narrowing areas of choice, until they reached a focus first in Abraham, and then in the choice of the people by God in Egypt and their delivery. At five points in those early chapters (Gn 2:4; 5:1; 6:9; 11:10; 11:27) the process of choice is carefully set out. God is active throughout his creation, but his particular purpose of salvation is to be seen in the creating, first of the whole universe, then of Adam, then of Noah, then of Shem, and finally, from Shem's descendants, of Terah who is the ancestor of Abraham. There is a concentration of the divine power as God brings about the salvation which has been proved too hard for man to achieve.

At the centre of the narrowing series of choices the priest set the first expression of the unique relationship which God wishes to establish with man: the relationship of covenant. We shall have a great deal more to say about this later, but it is important to notice that its first occurrence is here at the beginning where the mind is still full

of the uncaused creative power. At the end of the
account of the flood, the priestly editor set a
covenant between God and Noah; and because
every human being except Noah and his family
had been destroyed, this covenant was a uni-
versal one, a promise made by God to the whole
human race:

> Then God said to Noah and to his sons with
> him, Behold, I establish my covenant with you
> and your descendants after you, and with
> every living creature that is with you, the birds,
> the cattle, and every beast of the earth with
> you, as many as came out of the ark. I estab-
> lish my covenant with you, that never again
> shall all flesh be cut off by the waters of a
> flood, and never again shall there be a flood to
> destroy the earth. [Gn 9:8–11]

And it ends with the remark that from Noah's
three sons 'the whole earth was peopled'. The
people of Israel may indeed have claimed a
choice and privilege beyond any other nation, but
their privilege was not an end in itself; it was to
be the means whereby all the world is brought
back to God. The point is established at the very
beginning.

And so the background is painted, the setting
is established, and Abraham appears on the
scene. It was no accident that he made the
journey from Mesopotamia to Palestine, but part
of the divine plan and in answer to the divine
call; the ultimate victory is already guaranteed:

But you, Israel, my servant,
   Jacob, whom I have chosen,
   the offspring of Abraham, my friend;
you whom I took from the ends of the earth,
   and called from its farthest corners,
saying to you, You are my servant,
   I have chosen you and not cast you off;
fear not, for I am with you,
   be not dismayed, for I am your God;
I will strengthen you, I will help you,
   I will uphold you with my victorious right
      hand. [Is 41:8–10]

The shadow of the exodus is cast a long way
before it.

Palestine is a corridor country, a passage area
through which the main lines of communication
run, connecting together the two main areas of
the eastern end of the Mediterranean Sea. Only
since the cutting of the Suez Canal a hundred
years ago and, much more recently, the growth
in the use of air transport, has this changed. The
reason is simple. The area is dominated by two
great river valleys which have been cradles of
civilisation from the earliest times for which we
have evidence. To the south the river Nile drains
the whole eastern half of Africa from the equator
to the Mediterranean. Rising in the complex of
great lakes which straddle the equator in
Uganda, it winds down through the Sudan and
the eastern end of the Sahara desert until it fans
out into the sprawling swamp of river mouths
and marshes which make up its delta, the place

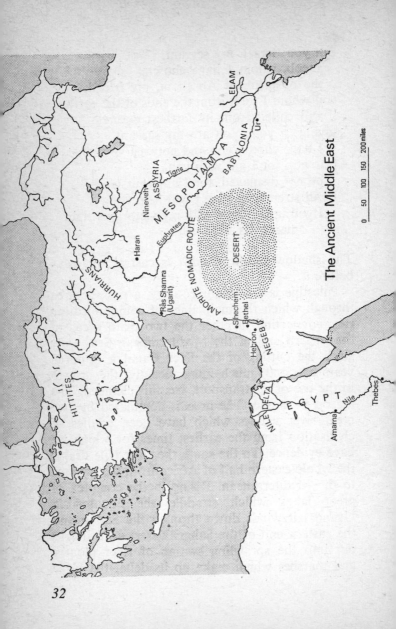

The Ancient Middle East

0   50   100   150   200 miles

32

where it finally enters the sea. Quite literally, for a good deal of its journey it flows through desert. In places the fertile, cultivated strip along its banks is no more than a mile across from waste sand to waste sand, and that narrow ribbon of green is only preserved at the cost of ceaseless labour with irrigation channels and unending control of the precious water flowing in them. Yet the people who drained the marshes and dug the channels and learned to live with the great river formed one of the greatest civilisations the world has known. Its history was already more than three thousand years old when Christ was born, and the buildings by which it is best known, the pyramid tombs of the kings of the Third and Fourth Dynasties, had been standing for more than two thousand five hundred years.

The river Nile was the backbone of the country, the only real unifying factor, and the people's main god. Its water, and the mud it left behind when it returned to its channel after the annual floods from the Ethiopian mountains, turned the desert into rich agricultural land. Despite the cataracts by which the river was broken, it was the only means of communication between the broad fertile lands of the delta on the Mediterranean coast, the long strip of river, and the area dominated by Thebes, a thousand miles up the Nile. It is no wonder that the history of the country is dominated by the rivalry between the delta people and the Thebans.

To the east of Palestine the other great river complex, the area drained by the Tigris and

Euphrates rivers, formed the other great cradle of civilisations. The Greeks later called it 'the land between the rivers'—Mesopotamia—and so it has remained. On the far side, the eastern side, Mesopotamia is contained by a long mountainous region stretching from Iran (where it joins onto the Himalayas) right across to Turkey. It is an area of lakes and mountains and high plateaus, with Mount Ararat as one of the highest. Around 2000 BC it was peopled by Hurrians and Hittites living each in loosely organised federations. Down in the great river plain itself, around the northern part of the Tigris, the Assyrians lived round their capital of Nineveh. Although they were the ancestors of the dreaded military power who struck such terror into the Jews and their neighbours, it was to be more than a thousand years before that took place. Around 2000 BC they were commercially important but little more. Further down, towards the Persian Gulf, came Sumerians, whose most important town at that time was Ur, on the river Euphrates, although the area is usually called Babylonia, after the town later to become so famous, a little higher up river. The people of this area are sometimes called Chaldeans. For a time they dominated the area, but it was never a very well organised control, and one after another, the outlying parts broke away from them until, finally, Ur came to an end when it was overthrown by its eastern neighbour, Elam. It is of interest to us because it was shortly after this, according to the

last few verses of Gn 11, that Abraham left Ur
for Palestine:

> Terah took Abram his son and Lot the son of
> Haran, his grandson, and Sarai his daughter-
> in-law, his son Abram's wife, and they went
> forth together from Ur of the Chaldeans to go
> into the land of Canaan; but when they came
> to Haran, they settled there. [Gn 11:31]

The pattern of power in Mesopotamia was constantly moving and changing at this time, compared with the comparative stability of Egypt,
for a number of reasons. For one thing, there was
nothing to compare with the single thread of
unity the Nile gave Egypt; the Tigris–Euphrates
basin is a wide area where there was ample opportunity for locally distinctive ways of life.
Then to either side of the Nile was the protection
of the desert; behind Mesopotamia, on the other
hand, the mountains harboured hostile tribes and
even, on occasion, poured out floods of migrating
peoples when population movements in the Rus-
sian steppe country pressed through the Cau-
casus. But equally important for us were a people
who lived in the semi-desert conditions to the
west of Mesopotamia: the Amorites.

The country lying directly between Babylonia
and Egypt was impassable desert, particularly in
those days before the camel had been domesti-
cated, but at the northern end of this Arabian
desert was a people who lived by grazing its
flocks on the sparse grass and moving on as soon
as the pastures had been eaten bare again. T. E.

Lawrence has written vividly, in *The Seven Pillars of Wisdom*, about the tides and circulations of the present-day nomad and semi-nomad Arabs. The settled agricultural lands have always proved an attraction, even when the austerity and discipline of the desert have provided the ideals and standards, and the weaker peoples have been pushed into the desert while the stronger have moved their flocks down into the areas of dependable pasture and even of the plough. So too with the Amorites. They penetrated into much of the Mesopotamian region and gained control for a while; Amorite rulers occupied nearly every throne in an area stretching from Palestine to the Persian Gulf. Moreover, they were Semites, the cultural and racial group to which the Jews belong. If we are to try to place Abraham amongst the peoples of his time (about 1800 BC) we are safest if we see him as an Amorite.

Abraham may have entered Palestine as a member of an Amorite group, as part of a population movement no different from many others. But the people who preserved the tradition, the scribes who wrote down the stories about Abraham which had already been told for centuries around the camp fires at the local sanctuaries, had the advantage of hindsight. They knew what the effects of that movement were, they knew something of the results that had flowed from Abraham's life. For Abraham was not just another Amorite taking his family and flocks along a well-trodden route of Amorite movement; he was the beginning of the nation, the father of the

people. Even that is not the whole of the story.
If he were merely the founder of the Jewish
nation his proper place would be at the beginning of the story, not in chapter 12. Before the
writer got to Abraham he had a lot to tell: the
whole story of mankind trying to live without
God. The arrival of Abraham in Canaan is the
climax of a story, not the beginning, and that
story is told in the opening chapters of Genesis:
man's rebellion against his maker, his betrayal
of the trust and privilege God had vested in him;
the descent into murder and squalor, and the
failure of mankind's attempts to undo the damage, symbolically, by its own efforts:

> Come, let us build ourselves a city, and a tower
> with its top in the heavens, and let us make a
> name for ourselves, lest we be scattered abroad
> upon the face of the whole earth. [Gn 11 : 4]

Only God could undo the damage caused by
man's disobedience, and the move of Abraham
from his homeland was the first step in God's
long work of restoration and re-creation which
reached its completion eighteen hundred years
later in the birth of Jesus Christ, and the cross
and resurrection.

Now the Lord said to Abram (Abraham is just
a lengthened form of the name), Go from your
country and your kindred and your father's
house to the land that I will show you. And I
will make of you a great nation, and I will bless
you, and make your name great, so that you
will be a blessing. I will bless those who bless

you, and him who curses you I will curse; and by you all the nations of the earth shall bless themselves. [Gn 12:1–3]

The call of Abraham is the clue to the early chapters of Genesis, and to the whole of the subsequent history of man's salvation, for there the pattern is established. The initiative is God's and the plan is God's, but for it to be successful it is essential that man co-operate with complete trust and obedience. This is the heart of faith: not a mere intellectual assent to a set of propositions, still less a passive acceptance of God's existence and of the world as it is, but an active submission to God's love, an active search to find what his will is, and an active obedience which is undismayed by the difficulties which appear. For it is not man's power which is engaged, but God's, and things are possible for God which are beyond man. It is for this reason that Abraham has been seen by both Jews and Christians as the great example of the man of faith. The simple account of Abraham's actions breathes precisely the same spirit as St Luke's account of the Annunciation:

And Mary said to the angel, How can this be, since I have no husband? And the angel said to her,
    The Holy Spirit will come upon you,
    and the power of the Most High will overshadow you;
    therefore the child to be born will be called holy,
    the Son of God.

38

And behold, your kinswoman Elizabeth in her old age has also conceived a son; and this is the sixth month with her who was called barren. For with God nothing will be impossible. And Mary said, Behold, I am the handmaid of the Lord; let it be to me according to your word. [Lk 1:34–38]

It is worth noticing that the extent of God's power is shown in a similar way with Abraham's wife Sarah as it was with Elizabeth, for although God promised Abraham that he would be the father of a great nation, his wife was barren.

The promise made to Abraham was a threefold one. First there is the promise that he will be the father of a great nation. It is natural that the nation's memory should preserve this as the main promise, but closely associated with it is a second factor, the promise of territory:

Then the Lord appeared to Abram, and said, To your descendants I will give this land. [Gn 12:7]

The possession of the land of Canaan, the Holy Land, was an enormously important element in the nation's consciousness of itself and of its vocation and privilege. The land became a sacrament of even more importance than the temple itself: it was the visible sign of God's power and of his favour, and indeed, it even became the sign of his presence amongst them, a belief which survived the destruction of Jerusalem and the exile to Babylon. But more important, seen within the context of the whole history of salvation, was the

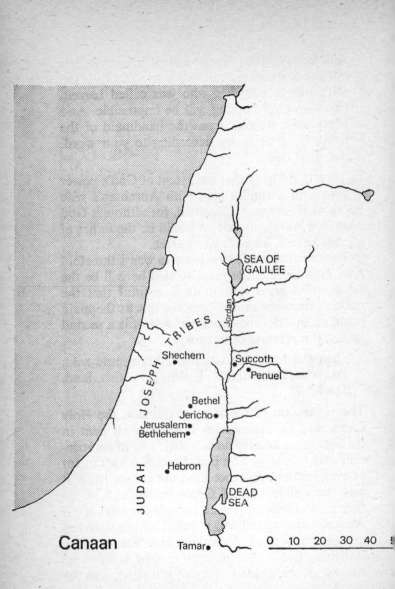

SEA OF
GALILEE

Jordan

JOSEPH TRIBES

Shechem

Succoth

Penuel

Bethel

Jericho

Jerusalem
Bethlehem

JUDAH

Hebron

DEAD
SEA

Canaan

Tamar

0 10 20 30 40 5

third element in the promise, that Abraham was to be the means whereby the whole world was to be brought within the area of God's blessing and peace. There had already been a hint of this, as we have seen, in the covenant made with Noah (Gn 9:9), but that particular story, although it may be very old, was not in fact added to the collection of Abraham stories until four hundred years after the collection we are now looking at, and by then the Jews had had the experience of the Babylonian exile to teach them that they must look beyond their own narrow community, so the earlier statement of this truth is much the more impressive. The heart of this promise is repeated in the stories of Isaac and of Jacob, Abraham's son and grandson (Gn 26:4; 28:13), and also, most importantly of all, to Moses after the escape from Egypt:

> And the Lord said to Moses, Depart, go up hence, you and the people whom you have brought up out of the land of Egypt, to the land of which I swore to Abraham, Isaac, and Jacob, saying, To your descendants I will give it. [Ex 33:1]

Here, again, we are in the same source, the same collection of stories, as the story of the call of Abraham and the promises made to him by God. Clearly, in the mind of the writer, Abraham's call and the escape of his descendants from Egypt are part of the same saving act of God's.

The land to which Abraham went was already occupied. It formed part of the narrow strip of fertile land between the Mediterranean Sea on the west, and the eastward barrenness of the Dead Sea and the Arabian desert; naturally such an area would be settled. Not only was it settled, to some extent it was under the control of Egypt. As the only corridor for communications between the western and eastern wings of the 'fertile crescent' (the continuous stretch of fertile land running down the Nile, along the eastern Mediterranean coast and through Mesopotamia) Canaan was bound to be an area of interest to both the Egyptians and the Mesopotamian powers, even at such an early time as this. The Mesopotamian area, as we have seen, was disorganised and to some extent sealed off by the Amorites, but the Egyptians had no such problem. Documents discovered at Râs Shamra (Ugarit) on the Mediterranean, and at Amarna in Egypt, show that Egypt kept control of the area, and particularly of the main roads, by means of subject kings who paid her tribute and could call on Egyptian troops in case of need. Abraham's move was not merely one of distance, he also moved into the Egyptian sphere of influence and control. So after he had established altars at Shechem and near Bethel, and journeyed into the southern coastal plain of the Negeb, it was natural that he should make for Egypt when a local famine burned the pastures and produced a food shortage. Returning from Egypt, he went first to the altar near Bethel again, and then moved to Hebron, the sanctuary which became so prominent under David. But all through these early stories of the fathers of the nation the geographical details are unimportant and, like some of the stories themselves, grew up as the reasons why sanctuaries existed at certain places, or even why there was ill-feeling between the Jews and some of their neighbours. Some of the details are bound to be mysterious to us, and some of them to be trivial, for we are no longer interested in some of the things the listeners wanted to know or enjoyed hearing as they listened to the priests telling the old, familiar stories round the sanctuary camp-fires. The points that matter are the relations between man and God, the attitude to God which these stories reveal. And all the time we must bear in mind that the narrative is moving steadily towards the escape from Egypt when God showed his power and made the great covenant with the people.

The most important section of the Abraham stories begins with chapter 15, and is concerned with the covenant between God and Abraham, and the miraculous conception of Isaac by the barren Sarah. Abraham protested that his heir would have to be one of his adopted sons, but God reassured him that he would have a son himself, and Abraham trusted him. God then entered into a covenant with him, using the form for the most solemn kind of covenant between men: animals are killed and cut into two pieces, then the participants walk between the pieces as a seal of their promise—and, possibly, an indication of the kind of curse they are prepared to accept if they are not faithful. Then, in a passage vivid with the experience of the numinous, the indescribable awe which accompanies God's presence, the promise was renewed:

> As the sun was going down, a deep sleep fell on Abram; and lo, a dread and great darkness fell upon him. Then the Lord said to Abram, Know of a surety that your descendants will be sojourners in a land that is not theirs, and will be slaves there, and they will be oppressed for four hundred years; but I will bring judgement on the nation which they serve, and afterwards they shall come out with great possessions... When the sun had gone down and it was dark, behold, a smoking fire pot and a flaming torch passed between these pieces. On that day the Lord made a covenant with Abram, saying, To your descendants I give this land, from the river of Egypt to the great river, the river Euphrates. [Gn 15:12–18]

There follows a section accounting for the mixed ancestry of the Jews' desert neighbours, the Bedouin, as the result of Abraham's attempt to secure God's promised heir by having a son by his wife's Egyptian servant, Hagar, and a later priestly section giving the origins of circumcision, but the main thread is taken up again in chapter 18. The intimacy between God and Abraham grew, and the promise that Abraham and Sarah would have a son is repeated, this time with a definite time attached to it and the firm statement that this would be a miracle (the Hebrew word for miracle means 'too hard'):

The Lord said, I will surely return to you in the
spring, and Sarah your wife shall have a son . . .
Now Abraham and Sarah were old, advanced
in age; it had ceased to be with Sarah after the
manner of women. So Sarah laughed to herself,
saying, After I have grown old, and my husband is old, shall I have pleasure? The Lord
said to Abraham, Why did Sarah laugh, and
say, Shall I indeed bear a child, now that I am
old? Is anything too hard for the Lord? At the
appointed time I will return to you, in the
spring, and Sarah shall have a son. But Sarah
denied, saying, I did not laugh; for she was
afraid. He said, No, but you did laugh. [Gn 18:
10–15]

And when the boy was born, as God had promised, Abraham called him Isaac, from the
Hebrew for laughter.

The promise had been fulfilled, and Abraham
had a son, life brought by God out of the deadness
of Sarah's womb. The first part of Abraham's
destiny, his place in God's plan as the father of a
great nation, was beginning to be fulfilled. Yet for
all that this was so utterly dependent on God's
power, for whom nothing is too hard, the plan
was not to be fulfilled without man's full co-
operation. For the foundation of it was love, not
might, and Abraham was given the opportunity
to show his love—and show it, moreover, as a
father prepared to give his only son as a sacrifice.
Not until the very moment when he had the knife
stretched over Isaac, over the boy through whom

he had been promised that the inheritance and God's salvation would be made available, was his hand arrested and a ram provided in his place. The opportunity had been given and taken, and Abraham had shown that his faith and his love were absolute:

> By myself I have sworn, says the Lord, because you have done this, and have not withheld your son, your only son, I will indeed bless you, and I will multiply your descendants as the stars of heaven and as the sand which is on the seashore. And your descendants shall possess the gate of their enemies, and by your descendants shall all the nations of the earth bless themselves, because you have obeyed my voice. [Gn 22:16–18]

The last word should go to St Paul, that 'Hebrew of Hebrews' who saw in Christ the fulfilment of the promises made to Abraham, and who saw in Abraham's faith the pattern of Christian faith:

> . . . for he is the father of us all, as it is written, I have made you the father of many nations— in the presence of the God in whom he believed, who gives life to the dead and calls into existence the things that do not exist . . . No distrust made him waver concerning the promise of God, but he grew strong in his faith as he gave glory to God, fully convinced that God was able to do what he had promised. That is why his faith was reckoned to him as righteousness. But the words, It was reckoned to him, were written not for his sake alone, but for ours also.

It will be reckoned to us who believe in him that raised from the dead Jesus our Lord, who was put to death for our trespasses and raised for our justification. [Rm 4:16–25]

In the folk memories of the Amorite who journeyed out of obscurity three thousand eight hundred years ago may be seen the insight of a people who sought for the true relationship between man and the God who made him, and who recognised it in Abraham.

Additional notes

The Old Testament

The first eleven chapters of the Book of Genesis form an introduction to the whole Old Testament. The main divisions are:

1:1 – 2:4a The 'Priestly' introduction, in the form of an account of the creation, written in Babylon about 500 BC.

2:4b – 3:24 An old 'J' introduction, in the form of an account of the creation of a man and a woman, their disobedience and its consequences.

4:1–15 The murder of Abel by Cain, 'J'.

4:16–26 The origins of various cities, tribes, and professions, in terms of Cain's descendants, 'J'.

5:1–32 (except 29) The 'Priestly' list of Adam's descendants. Verse 29 is the 'J' explanation of Noah's name.

6:1–4 A fragment of an old legend about the origins of ancient heroes, 'J'.

6:5–8; 7:1–5, 12, 16b, 17b (and 'forty days'), 22–23; 8:2b–3a, 6–12, 13b, 20–22 The 'J' account of the flood.

6:9–22; 7:6–11, 13–16, 17a, 18–21, 24; 8:1–2a, 3b–5, 13a, 14–19; 9:1–17 The 'Priestly' account of the flood.

9:18–29 An incident accounting for the subjugation of the Canaanites, 'J'.

10:1a, 2–7, 20, 22–23, 31–32 The 'Priestly' list of the nations in terms of Noah's descendants.

10:1b, 8–19, 21, 24–30 The 'J' list of the nations in terms of Noah's descendants.

11:1–9 The Tower of Babel: the origin of different languages, 'J'.

11:10–27, 31–32 The 'Priestly' account of Abraham's ancestors.

11:28–30 The 'J' account of Abraham's ancestors.

The 'J' tradition, up to the death of Abraham, is to be found in the following sections:

12:1–4a, 6–9, 10–20; 13:1–5, 6b–11a, 12b–18; 15:3–4, 6–15, 17–18; 16:1b–2, 4–8, 11–14; 18:1–33; 19:1–28, 30–38; 20:18; 21:1a, 2a, 7, 28–30, 33; 22:15–18, 20–24; 24:1–67; 25:1–5.

It must be emphasised that these lists of references will be misleading if they are thought of in too clear and definite a way. They give the difference between an early and late form of the tradition, rather than sections to which a clear date can be given. There is very little agreement amongst scholars about where the divisions should be made, and the old view that they represent documents which then remained unchanged has been very heavily criticised. The reader is referred to chapter 1 of this book.

Accounts of a covenant with Abraham:
12:1–3; 15:12–18; 17:1–9; 18:17–19; 22:16–18.

The New Testament

The main references to Abraham in the New Testament are:

Mt 1:1–17   Christ's descent is traced from Abraham.

Mt 22:32   The covenant with Abraham and his descendants is quoted by Christ as evidence for the resurrection.

Lk 19:9   Christ says that his first responsibility is to fulfil the promises made to Abraham's descendants.

Jn 8:33–47   Christ refutes the Jews who rest their security on their physical descent from Abraham. He tells them that if they really were Abraham's children they would have a faith like Abraham's and not try to kill him.

Ac 3:25   Peter tells the crowd that the covenant made with Abraham has at last been fulfilled.

Rm 4 (entire); Gal 3:6–29   Abraham's faith is given as the pattern of Christian faith.

Gal 4:21–31   The Christian's freedom from external legalism is compared with the rejection of Abraham's slave son, Ishmael (born of Hagar), and the miraculous birth of Isaac, Abraham's son by his wife Sarah.

Heb 7:1–10   Abraham's gifts to Melchizedek (Gn 14:17–20) are quoted to illustrate Christ's priesthood.

Heb 11:8–12   The faith of Abraham and Sarah is held up as an example.

You might like to consider: what effect human sin has on our own society and what solution the life and works of Christ have to offer; and whether there are people in our own time whose obedience to God has effects as far-reaching as Abraham's.

2

The Patriarchs

The key to the understanding of the Old Testament is the exodus, the escape from Egypt, for there the pattern of man's salvation is most clearly to be seen: the pouring out of power, unearned by man, undeserved, yet surrounding him with the might of God's love. And on man's part, co-operation with that power, recognition of it and trust in it. Sometimes the recognition was dim and the trust uncertain, but through all the twists and turns of the history God's purpose for his people could be seen driving forward.

It is against this background that the stories of the patriarchs must be seen: Abraham himself, of course, and, in the second half of the Book of Genesis from chapter 25 onwards, the stories of Abraham's son Isaac, Isaac's son Jacob (whose name at one stage was changed to Israel), and Jacob's twelve sons after most of whom the twelve tribes are named. Of Jacob's sons, Joseph occupies the centre of the stage, for it was through Joseph that the Jews went to live in Egypt. They entered Egypt as privileged immigrants, protected by the power Joseph had acquired and by the favour of the Pharaoh, and only in the course of generations did their condition deteriorate to the slavery of the time of Moses. Their knowledge of God's power, and their proud boast as his chosen people, was founded on their rescue from Egypt. And if the story of that rescue was to be told at all completely, it must tell how they came to be in Egypt in the first place. This is the thread that runs all through the stories of the patriarchs, the end towards which they move, the conclusion which gives them their unity.

As we have seen, the account as we now have it in our bibles is the result of centuries of meditation and reflection, and the skilful stitching together of stories and comments from many different sources. In what follows we shall mainly be following one particular strand, the earliest to contain a connected collection of stories and incidents covering the whole range of the history. It is usually called by the letter 'J' because it uses the Hebrew name 'Yahweh' for God all the way through, and at one time scholars thought this should be written 'Jehovah'. The other sources thought Yahweh was a name God did not reveal to his people until the time of Moses, and until that point is reached in the history they use 'Elohim' or 'El Shaddai'. In some ways 'J' seems to reflect the interests of the southern of the two parts into which the Hebrew kingdom split after the death of Solomon, the kingdom of Judah. But although it is the earliest of the strands to reach the written form in which we now know it, this does not mean that it is just a collection of naïve stories undisturbed by theological considerations. The collection was not written down until at least three hundred years after the exodus itself: three hundred years of telling and retelling the stories until their position in the pattern of God's great act of salvation became clear. They were told and arranged by people looking back at the central act of their salvation, at the moment when they were called out and chosen and made the people of God, and they were remembered and told precisely because they illuminated that fact. In some ways there is a parallel here with the earlier parts of the gospels, where events and sayings take on a new significance when we realise that they are leading up to the cross and resurrection.

The people who preserved and arranged these stories of their ancestors before their entry into Egypt, and the unknown writer who collected them and wrote them down, had a deep and mature faith in God, and a profound insight into his way with the men whom he calls to work with him. They knew that God was active in their nation's history, and that by his acts in history he had made himself known to them. More important, they saw that they were real men that God worked with, men moved by selfishness and lust and greed and anger and jealousy, and yet that he worked his will in his world through them. We are shocked, often, by some of the stories told of those early Israelites; they are told not because the men in them are examples of respectability but because the power of God is to be seen at work in their lives. We are sometimes tempted to feel that we would like to leave out of the New Testament some of the things we do not like about the apostles: their arguments about who was the greatest amongst them, or Paul's quarrel with Barnabas and Mark, and so too, indeed, with some of the stories of the patriarchs:

> And Sarah said to Abram, May the wrong done to me be on you! I gave my maid to your embrace, and when she saw that she had conceived, she looked on me with contempt. May the Lord judge between you and me! But Abram said to Sarah, Behold, your maid is in your power; do to her as you please. Then Sarah dealt harshly with her, and she fled from her. [Gn 16:5–6]

Yet the motive is near the heart of the salvation history: Abraham's need of an heir while Sarah is barren, for Abraham had been told by God that the promises would be fulfilled through his son.

God's plan was to be fulfilled through these men's descendants, and it was to be fulfilled in the land of Canaan, Palestine, the Holy Land. Their descendants would be given possession of this land by God, and—this the teller of the tale and his audience knew—God would do it by rescuing them from Egypt and leading them through the desert back to the place where the promises were first given. There is a most satisfying completeness and simplicity, almost inevitability, about it all.

Abraham arranged Isaac's marriage from amongst his own people, sending a servant back to Nahor in Mesopotamia, and the servant returned with Rebekah. Whatever the motive for avoiding marriage with the local Canaanites, whether religious, or to avoid property passing to another race, Abraham was insistent that the girl must come to Isaac, for Isaac was not going to leave Canaan:

> Abraham said to him, See to it that you do not take my son back there. The Lord, the God of heaven, who took me from my father's house and from the land of my birth, and who spoke to me and swore to me, To your descendants I will give this land, he will send his angel before you, and you shall take a wife for my son from there. But if the woman is not willing to follow you, then you will be free from this oath of mine; only you must not take my son back there. [Gn 24:6–8]

In the event, Rebekah needed no urging, but went with the servant the day after he had seen her, despite her family's quite natural suggestion that she should wait a day or two. The presence of the heir in his inheritance was maintained; that the danger was real is shown by Isaac's son, Jacob: it took him seven years to get Rachel away from her father, Rebekah's brother Laban.

With Isaac and Rebekah the pattern of life brought out of death, which had emerged from Abraham's struggles to get an heir, was repeated:

> And Isaac prayed to the Lord for his wife, because she was barren. [Gn 25:21]

But this time there was to be no long wait before God's intervention. Rebekah conceived and twins were born, Esau and Jacob. A further variation of

God's initiative was to be shown through them: although Esau was the elder of the twins, the inheritance was to go to Jacob and the law of the rights of the firstborn be set aside. St Paul, writing to the Romans, saw in this a proof of God's intervention, a sign that he was active at every stage and in every detail of the history of salvation:

> ... when Rebekah had conceived children by our forefather Isaac, though they were not yet born and had done nothing either good or bad, in order that God's purpose of election might continue, not because of works but because of his call, she was told, The elder will serve the younger. [Rm 9:11–12]

But although the initiative was indeed God's, there was another factor, the attitude of Esau and Jacob themselves. At this stage, Jacob emerges from the stories as a thief and a liar who, encouraged and helped by Rebekah, robbed Esau of his birthright and deceived his father, blind in his old age.

The story turns on the power of a father's blessing. For the Hebrews it conferred authority and prosperity, a cross between a will and the legal transfer of power. Combined with this there is something of the power of the prophetic word— not so much a seeing into the future, but a *making* of the future by the words which are spoken about it. It is close to the effectiveness of an authoritative command. Naturally, Isaac's blessing would go to his eldest son, Esau, even if no more than a few minutes separated him from the younger,

Jacob. It is this that Jacob wanted: the blessing conferring upon him the inheritance of God's promises:

When Isaac was old and his eyes were dim so that he could not see, he said, Behold I am old; I do not know the day of my death. Now then, take your weapons, your quiver and your bow, and go out to the field and hunt game for me, that I may bless you before I die. So when Esau went to the field to hunt for game and bring it, Rebekah said to her son Jacob, I heard your father speak to your brother Esau, Bring me game, and prepare for me savoury food, that I may eat it. Then Rebekah took the best garments of Esau her elder son, which were with her in the house, and put them on Jacob her younger son. And Isaac said, Who are you, my son? Jacob said to his father, I am Esau your first-born. I have done as you told me; now sit up and eat of my game, that you may bless me. But Isaac said to his son, How is it that you have found it so quickly, my son? He answered, because the Lord your God granted me success. And Isaac said, Are you really my son Esau? He answered, I am. Then he said, Bring it to me, that I may eat of my son's game and bless you. So he brought it to him, and he ate; and he brought him wine, and he drank. Then his father Isaac said to him, Come near me and kiss me, my son. So he came near and kissed him; and he smelled the smell of his garments, and blessed him, and said,

> See, the smell of my son
>> is as the smell of a field which the Lord has
>> blessed!
> Let peoples serve you,
>> and nations bow down to you.
> Cursed be every one who curses you,
>> and blessed be every one who blesses you!

Esau returned, of course, from his hunting, and the deception was discovered. The unexpanded version of the story, as recorded by the 'J' source, ends on the authentic note of high tragedy:

> When Esau heard the words of his father, he cried out with an exceedingly great and bitter cry, and said to his father, Bless me, even me also, O my father! [Gn 27:1–34 sections]

Yet the point is worth noting, when we have finished feeling sorry for Esau, that Jacob had indeed shown how much he valued the blessing, the inheritance. The inheritance of God's promises was the most important thing in the world to him, more important than any material wealth, for the immediate consequence was that he had to flee from the country, penniless, to escape from Esau's anger. He fled to Laban, Rebekah's brother, where he fell in love with Rachel, and since he was unable to raise the cost of the bride price, he was forced to work for Laban for seven years. Jacob did become wealthy in time (and by some very shady tricks with Laban's flocks, as we might expect), but it was entirely by his own efforts and not through any property inherited from Isaac.

Jacob gave up everything for the sake of the promises of God, and despite his unsatisfactory character, one begins to see why he is held up as the man from whom the nation took its name, the father of the founders of the twelve tribes. The promise which God had made to Abraham he repeated to Isaac; the account locates the incident at Beer-sheba, near the southernmost extent of the Holy Land:

And the Lord appeared to him the same night and said, I am the God of Abraham your father; fear not, for I am with you and will bless you and multiply your descendants for my servant Abraham's sake. [Gn 26:24]

The god-given right to live in the area was recognised at the same time by the local king, Abimelech, for he and Isaac made a covenant not to molest each other.

But the real interest of the story is with Jacob, once Abraham was dead; Isaac is little more than a necessary link conveying the blessing from Abraham to Jacob. In his exile, working for Laban at Haran, Jacob obtained Rachel for a wife, and it will be no surprise that she, too, the third in succession of wives of the promise, was barren. But by a succession of women, Leah, Rachel's elder sister, and two of Rachel's maids, Jacob had ten sons, Reuben, Simeon, Levi, Judah, Dan, Naphtali, Gad, Asher, Issachar and Zebulun, before Rachel herself conceived and bore Joseph. The significance of Joseph's position is marked out from the beginning in the narrative,

58

for he was the first-born of Jacob and his legitimate wife Rachel. In time, Jacob asked Laban's permission to return to Canaan, and after a lot of complicated bargaining, in which Laban was outwitted, and what looks like a chase by Laban and his sons, Jacob approached the Jordan valley and his long-feared meeting with his brother Esau.

This is the context, the situation, for the most mysterious of all the incidents involving God and men in the Book of Genesis—one is almost tempted to say in the whole Old Testament. Jacob, forced to flee from the inheritance which he had obtained by a trick, and yet the one through whom the promises of God were to pass to his whole people, was at the point of return. He was the last of the single links in the chain, for after him the promise would descend through his twelve sons. He had sent servants ahead with gifts to placate Esau, and now, at night, he supervised his family and servants and goods as the caravan crossed one of the tributaries of the Jordan. He came last, and as he crossed the deep gully he found his way barred by a man, and the two of them fought in the darkness through the night:

> The same night he arose and took his two wives, his two maids and his eleven children, and sent them across the stream, and likewise everything that he had. And Jacob was left alone; and a man wrestled with him until the breaking of the day. When the man saw that he did not prevail against Jacob, he touched the hollow of his thigh; and Jacob's thigh was put

out of joint as he wrestled with him. Then he said, Let me go, for the day is breaking. But Jacob said, I will not let you go, unless you bless me. And he said to him, What is your name? And he said, Jacob. Then he said, Your name shall no more be called Jacob, but Israel, for you have striven with God and with men, and have prevailed. Then Jacob asked him, Tell me, I pray, your name. But he said, Why is it that you ask my name? And there he blessed him. And Jacob called the name of the place Peniel, saying, For I have seen God face to face, and yet my life is preserved. [Gn 32: 22–30]

Whatever primitive beliefs may have originally gone into the making of this story, the main question to ask is what place it has in the events leading up to the exodus. Seen in this light, several points emerge. Jacob exerted his considerable strength through the night not, it seems, because the way was denied him, but because he wanted a blessing. Then the stranger changed his name from Jacob, which literally means 'he takes by the heel' or 'he supplants', with its dishonourable associations, to 'Israel'. The basic meaning of 'Israel' is 'May God rule' or 'God strives'. He gave Jacob the blessing he asked, after refusing to tell him his own name (which would imply, for a Hebrew, revealing his whole character and even, perhaps, putting himself into his power), and, finally, Jacob named the place 'Peniel': 'The face of God'. Seen in this light, the incident became a deep reassurance to Jacob that the inheritance really was his, and at the same time a test of how far he was still prepared to exert himself for it: 'But Jacob said, I will not let you go, unless you bless me.' When we realize that the person whom he was addressing was no less than God himself, the simple words become a great act of faith. Jacob entered his inheritance with the blessing confirmed.

On the surface, Jacob's meeting with Esau appears to be filled with brotherly love and the pleasure of meeting each other again, but we may perhaps detect a more ominous note in Esau's offer to accompany Jacob to his destination at Succoth on the river Jordan; when this was declined he suggested leaving some of his men, and this too Jacob refused with the words, 'What need is there? Let me find favour in the sight of my lord.' So Esau went back to his own territory south of the Dead Sea. In the end, Jacob moved to Bethel, and then on to Bethlehem. At Bethlehem, as a sign that the promise and blessings were effective, Rachel bore him his last son, Benjamin, the only one of his twelve sons to be born in the Holy Land, and died giving birth to him. Rachel was buried at Bethlehem. Centuries later, during the siege of Jerusalem by the Babylonians, Jeremiah wrote of her weeping for her children, killed or taken into slavery, for the district where she was buried was already occupied; and Jeremiah's words were used by St Matthew to comment on the slaughter of the children of Bethlehem by Herod when he was trying to kill the child Jesus:

A voice is heard in Ramah,
lamentation and bitter weeping.
Rachel is weeping for her children;
she refuses to be comforted for her children,
because they are not.
Thus says the Lord:
Keep your voice from weeping,
and your eyes from tears;
for your work shall be rewarded, says the Lord,
and they shall come back from the land of
the enemy.
There is hope for your future, says the Lord,
and your children shall come back to their
own country. [Jer 31:15–17]

The final great block of stories, the Joseph saga, occupies the last part of the Book of Genesis from chapter 37 to the end. The main purpose of the stories is to show how the Hebrews came to be living in Egypt, but they are full of delight quite apart from their place in the whole plan of Genesis: the resentment of the ten elder brothers at Jacob's favouring of Joseph, his enslavement in Egypt and imprisonment through refusing to sleep with his employer's wife, his delivery from prison through the ability to interpret Pharaoh's dreams and predict the approaching famine, his rise to wealth and authority, and the cat-and-mouse game he played with his brothers when they came to Egypt to buy food.

There is a lot of contradiction and repetition in the Joseph stories; some of this will be caused by their popularity. Altogether they have the length and quality of a novelette; they must have delighted the audience, particularly the northern kingdom audiences who traced their ancestry from Joseph. We may be sure that they lost nothing in the telling. But the complexity is also in part caused by the amalgamation of the two earlier traditions and, in places, the late priestly tradition as well. The main theological interest, however, and that a very considerable one, lies in a few verses towards the end of the Joseph stories: the section which describes Jacob (whose other name, remember, is Israel) blessing Joseph's sons, Manasseh and Ephraim. The section is Gn 48 : 8–20. It is mainly taken from the 'J' collection of stories.

A glance at a map which shows where the tribes eventually settled in the Holy Land, according to the tradition of the conquest given in the books of Joshua and Judges, will help much in making sense of Jacob's blessing of Joseph's sons. The twelve tribes all had their place in various parts of the country, but the key positions were taken by Judah in the south, and by Ephraim and Manasseh in the north. It does not matter how far this is historically accurate; what does matter is the beliefs of the people who formed the stories and listened to them. Where one might expect to see the name Joseph occur we find, instead, the names of his two sons, and their names sprawl across the bulk of what was later to become the northern kingdom. Clearly, they meant a lot to very many of the people, the ones who traced their descent from them. It is against this background that we must see Jacob's blessing.

For it is more than a blessing: it is an adoption.
All the other tribes were named after Jacob's
sons: the two named after grandsons of his have
the legitimacy of it confirmed. Jacob adopted
them as his sons:

> ... in them let my name be perpetuated, and
> the name of my fathers Abraham and Isaac.
> [Gn 48:16]

If we can be clear about this aspect it will leave
us free to look closely at the rest of the event. It is
a remarkable statement of faith.

Joseph brought his two children in to the blind
Jacob and first he greeted them and fondled them
as any grandfather would his grandchildren,
especially as this strand of the tradition implies
that Jacob had not met them before:

> When Israel saw Joseph's sons, he said, Who
> are these? ('Saw' here only implies 'met'.)
> Joseph said to his father, They are my sons,
> whom God has given me here. And he said,
> Bring them to me, I pray you, that I may bless
> them. Now the eyes of Israel were dim with age,
> so that he could not see. So Joseph brought
> them near him; and he kissed them and em-
> braced them. And Israel said to Joseph, I had
> not thought to see your face (again); and lo,
> God has let me see your children also. [Gn 48:
> 8–11]

Joseph then placed the boys ready for Jacob's
blessing, and because there was a belief that a

blessing conferred with the right hand was more powerful than one given with the left, he placed the elder boy, Manasseh, under Jacob's right hand and the younger, Ephraim, under the left one. To his surprise—and annoyance—Jacob crossed his hands, and nothing Joseph could say or do would stop his father getting it wrong:

> When Joseph saw that his father laid his right hand on the head of Ephraim, it displeased him; and he took his father's hand, to remove it from Ephraim's head to Manasseh's head. And Joseph said to his father, Not so, my father; for this one is the first-born; put your right hand upon his head.

But the infuriating old man knew what he was doing:

> But his father refused, and said, I know, my son, I know; he also shall become a people, and he also shall be great; nevertheless his younger brother shall be greater than he, and his descendants shall become a multitude of nations. [Gn 48:17–19]

No doubt we may see here the influence of the later political supremacy of Ephraim, but we must remember that Jacob himself was a younger son who obtained a greater blessing than his elder brother, Esau, and always there is the overriding principle that the blessing falls on those whom God chooses, not necessarily on those who have the legal right. 'The first shall be last, and the last first,' said Jesus.

The blessing was in three parts. The first part established the continuity of the religious experience through three generations:

The God before whom my fathers Abraham and Isaac walked. [Gn 48:15]

Jacob had himself added to that experience, and the descendants of those whom he was blessing would use it to interpret the events in Egypt when God showed them how great his power is. This was no static inheritance, no dead creed whose power all lay in the past; it would be the principle by which God's hand was to be seen active all down through their history.

The second part invoked the continual creative power of God poured out into his creation:

The God who has led me all my life long to this day. [Gn 48:15]

The image is that of a shepherd: the eastern shepherd who leads, rather than drives, his flock. It was a natural image for a nation of nomadic shepherds, and an image which has been sanctified by Jesus's use of it:

... the sheep hear his voice, and he calls his own sheep by name and leads them out. When he has brought out all his own, he goes before them, and the sheep follow him, for they know his voice ... I am the good shepherd ... [Jn 10: 3–11]

Two defective ideas about God are common amongst us nowadays. One sees him as no more than the originator of the universe, a workman who put his tools away when he had finished his work and walked away from it and left it. This view sees no continuing dependence of the creation on God, no need for his continual power sustaining the universe and holding it in being. The other view gets a little further, but not very far. This thinks of God as a visitor, a power which intervenes from time to time in the world's history and retires again. The steady sequence of cause and effect has been interrupted, possibly redirected, but it is now left to go steadily on again. Neither view would have made sense to a Hebrew. Their belief was that God was with them, present and active all the time. Sometimes the effects of his presence were easier to see than at other times, but he was there whether he was seen or not. So Isaiah gave the reluctant King Ahaz God's sign: the child Immanuel—'God is with us', and Jesus confirmed it when he promised his disciples that he would be with them always, even to the end of the world. Jacob's simple statement is the essence of the Hebrew faith, God present and continually guiding his people, for they depend upon him.

Finally, in this blessing, Jacob invoked God as his closest relative ('the angel' here refers to God, as is shown by the parallelism with the other sections of the blessing):

The angel who has redeemed me from all evil, bless the lads. [Gn 48:16]

The key to this is to be found in the Hebrew law about the responsibility of the members of a family towards each other. In law no Hebrew could possess another Hebrew as a slave, though in practice this was flouted. But there were others than Hebrews living in the country, and if a man ran himself into debt with one of these foreigners he might find he had to sell himself into slavery to pay the debt. It was then the urgent duty of the man's relatives to buy his freedom—and he should only have remained a slave if all his family were so poor that they could not raise the price of his 'redemption':

> If a stranger or sojourner with you becomes rich, and your brother beside him becomes poor and sells himself to the stranger or sojourner with you, or to a member of the stranger's family, then after he is sold he may be redeemed: one of his brothers may redeem him, or his uncle, or his cousin may redeem him, or a near kinsman belonging to his family may redeem him . . . [Lv 25:47–48]

To Jacob, God was the close relative to whom he could turn when he was in trouble. More, he was the only one who could release him from the power of evil. What an anticipation there is here of the work of Jesus, and a fitting antithesis to the theme with which the book of Genesis opens: the disobedience of man and the turning of human hearts towards evil:

> The Lord saw that the wickedness of man was great in the earth, and that every imagination of the thoughts of his heart was only evil continually. [Gn 6:5]

The blessing is complete.

So far there has been no hint that the migration of the Hebrews to Egypt was anything but a great stroke of good fortune, made possible solely by the privileged position and protective hand of Joseph. Twice now, at the death of Jacob and again at the death of Joseph, a hint is given of the wonders to come, and of the need for God's power to be exerted in an exceptional way:

> I am about to die; but God will visit you, and bring you up out of this land to the land which he swore to Abraham, to Isaac, and to Jacob. [Gn 50:24. See also 48:21]

How far the stories in the Book of Genesis are to be taken literally, it is impossible to say. The accounts have reached us only after centuries of being handed on by the spoken and the written word; there is no knowing what modifications have been made to them in the process. But although we may hesitate before we accept them as the history of Abraham, Isaac, and Jacob, there is one thing of which we can be absolutely certain. They are the accurate testimony of the faith of a people at a very early stage in their history. The beliefs we have been looking at so far were held five hundred years before Socrates and Plato, four hundred years before the foundation of the republican form of government in Rome, and nine hundred years before the Roman landings in Britain. And even this is to take a late date for the mature formation of the Hebrew faith, a date after the death of David. Abraham, Isaac, and Jacob may become shadowy figures as we examine the stories about them, but the faith of the people who told those stories was no shadowy thing. It was rock hard, and every year of their nation's history opened out fresh insights into it. It was rock hard because they based it on a historical event: an event so extraordinary that it could only be the work of God, the proof that he had chosen them and that his protecting hand was with them in every turn of their history. That event was the exodus, and it is to this that we must now turn.

Additional notes

The Old Testament

The 'J' tradition, from the death of Abraham, is to be found in the following passages of Genesis:

25:11b, 18, 21–25a, 26a, 28; 26:1–3a, 6–14, 16–17, 19–33; 27:1a, 2–3, 4b, 5b–7a, 15, 18b–20, 24–27, 29ac, 31b–34, 41b–42, 43b, 45a; 28:10, 13–16, 19, 21b; 29:2–14, 26, 31–35; 30:3b–16, 22c–23a, 24–25, 27, 29–31a, 34–38a, 39–40ac, 41–43; 31:1, 3, 10, 12b, 15, 17–18a, 31, 43–44, 46, 48, 50a; 32:3–7a, 13b–22a, 23b, 24–29, 31–32; 33:1–17; 34:2b–3ac, 5, 7, 11, 19, 26, 29b–31; 35:14, 16–22a; 36:32–39; 37:2b, 2d–4, 12–13a, 14b, 18b, 21, 25b–27, 28b, 32a, 33b, 35; 38:1–30; 39:1–4a, 4c–5, 6b, 7b–23; 41:31, 34, 35b, 36b, 41–45a, 46b–49, 56a, 57; 42:2, 4–5, 7ac, 27–28a, 38; 43:1–13, 15–34; 44:1–34; 45:1a, 2b, 4–5ac, 9–11, 13–14, 19a–21a, 28; 46:1a, 28–34; 47:1–4, 6b, 12–27a, 29–31; 48:2b, 9b–10a, 13–19; 49:1b–24a, 27, 33b; 50:1–11, 14, 18, 21, 24.

The covenants with Isaac and Jacob will be found in 26:4 and 28:13.

There is a parallel between the patriarchs, through whom the Jews inherited the promises made with Abraham, Isaac, and Jacob, and the apostles. There are a number of allusions to this in the New Testament. Amongst these are:

Lk 6:13–16   Christ chooses the twelve.
Mk 6:7–13   The apostles are given authority and sent out to preach and heal.
Jn 30:21–23   Christ gives the apostles the same authority as he himself received from God the Father.
Mt 16:13–20   Peter recognises Jesus as the messiah and is given authority.
Jn 6:66–69   The apostles' statement of their faith in Christ is parallel with the single-mindedness of Jacob.

You might like to consider: whether the organisation and authority of the church meet our needs as successfully as the patriarchs and apostles met the needs of their times.

3

Egypt

The Book of Exodus opens with the ominous words (continuing to select the Yahwist's account of the events):

> And Joseph died, and all his brothers, and all that generation. And there arose a new king over Egypt, who did not know Joseph. [Ex 1:6, 8]

The protection, and the memory of it, had ended. With the ending of the protection the resentment of a nation for foreigners in their midst was released, and the traditional hostility of an agricultural people for a shepherd people contributed to this resentment. The story of the arrival and settlement of the Israelites in Egypt carries a hint of it:

> When Pharaoh calls you, and says, What is your occupation? you shall say, Your servants have been keepers of cattle from our youth even until now, both we and our fathers—in order that you may dwell in the land of Goshen; for every shepherd is an abomination to the Egyptians. [Gn 46:33–34]

It seems, indeed, that it was even difficult to find Egyptians with the necessary skill to look after cattle, for after giving the newly arrived Israelites permission to settle in Goshen, Pharaoh asked if there were any able men amongst them who could be put in charge of his herds (Gn 47:6). That may well be the happy thought of a later story-teller, but it underlines a real difference of skills and a source of hostility. Goshen was the area at the eastern end of the Nile delta, near the coast.

The new Pharaoh found that the foreigners had prospered and increased to the point where they might be a danger to the state in time of war, and it is worth noticing that Goshen lay across the main road to the north, the road Egyptian armies took and the only possible point from which Egypt might herself expect to be attacked. The Hebrews were in a strategic position, and they were aliens. Our own generation will need no explanation of how a feeling of hostility might grow towards them:

> Behold, the people of Israel are too many and too mighty for us. Come, let us deal shrewdly with them, lest they multiply, and, if war befall us, they join our enemies and fight against us . . . [Ex 1:9–10]

So the Egyptians set the Israelites to work with the objects of controlling them, of arresting their growth in numbers, and of benefiting from the building programme on which they employed them. The account names two store cities, Pithom and Raamses, as the result of their labours; they have both been identified as sites lying on the borders of Goshen and astride the military route out of Egypt. Possibly they were for military stores.

If the Yahwist had anything to say about Moses' birth and youth, we are not given it. His collection emerges again in the narrative at verse 11 of chapter 2 with Moses as a grown man. The slightly later collection of stories associated with the northern kingdom, the E source, tells of the edict to murder all male Hebrew children, either at birth or by drowning, and how Moses was rescued by Pharaoh's daughter, adopted by her, and brought up at court.

The critical step, which led to the experience in the desert by which God revealed his intention of rescuing the Israelites from their hardships, came accidentally. The adult Moses came across an Egyptian overseer ill-treating a Hebrew, and he killed him. His own people then blackmailed him when he tried to intervene in a fight between two Hebrews:

> One day, when Moses had grown up, he went out to his people and looked on their burdens; and he saw an Egyptian beating a Hebrew, one of his people. He looked this way and that, and seeing no one he killed the Egyptian and hid him in the sand. When he went out the next day, behold, two Hebrews were struggling together; and he said to the man who did wrong, Why do you strike your fellow? He answered, Who made you a prince and a judge over us? Do you mean to kill me as you killed the Egyptian? Then Moses was afraid, and thought,

> Surely the thing is known. When Pharaoh heard
> of it, he sought to kill Moses. [Ex 2:11–15]

The only solution was to flee, and Moses made for
the eastern desert, the Sinai peninsula:

> But Moses fled from Pharaoh, and stayed in the
> land of Midian. [Ex 2:15]

There, he came into contact with a Midianite priest
named Jethro, and married one of his daughters,
and Jethro is indeed an interesting person.

At this point it is worth doing some detective
work to find what Jethro's background was. First,
a very small point but an irritating one, there is
some confusion about the name given to this
Midianite priest, and it is well to recognise that
the confusion is there. Ex 2:18 calls him Reuel,
but it looks as if this is a mistake made by a scribe
when he was copying this section. Most likely,
Ex 2:18 did not give the man a name, but just
had, 'When they came to their father, he said . . .'
and so on. The mistake would have occurred because the scribe remembered a place in the Book
of Numbers (Nm 10:29) where the name of Moses'
father-in-law is given. Unfortunately there is room
for misunderstanding here, for the passage reads:
'And Moses said to Hobab the son of Reuel the
Midianite, Moses' father-in-law . . .' and the scribe
put the wrong name into the Exodus text he was
copying—a good example of trying to be helpful
and only confusing matters. He put in Reuel
where he should have put in Hobab, if he had to
put in anything at all. Hobab is a name used in

only one other place in the Old Testament (i.e., Jg 4:11): the name most commonly used for the man is Jethro, and this is the one we shall now use—for no one seems to be able to discover which of the two names, Hobab or Jethro, is the more correct.

Jethro appears twice: here, before the exodus itself, and again after the crossing of the Red Sea. The bible says that he was a priest, but it does not give us the name of his god, a surprising omission. The man who was the priest of the region where Moses had his first great experience of God, and where God told him that he intended to take the people out of Egypt under Moses' leadership, is naturally of great interest to us. In fact, as we might expect, the evidence suggests that Jethro's god was no less than Yahweh himself, the God of the Hebrews and the one who was about to demonstrate his power and his love for them so unmistakably. If this is so, the Midianite group would be an appropriate place for God to declare himself to Moses.

The evidence is by no means conclusive, but it all points in the same direction. Jethro was not only a Midianite, he was also a Kenite, as two references in the Book of Judges show:

And the descendants of the Kenite, Moses' father-in-law, went up with the people of Judah from the city of palms . . . [Jg 1:16]

and later in the book, there is an incident when one of the Kenite group strikes out on his own:

Now Heber the Kenite had separated from the

Kenites, the descendants of Hobab the father-in-law of Moses. . . . [Jg 4:11]

Both of these belong to the Yahwist source we have mainly been using so far. The point about the Kenites is that they were Yahweh worshippers although, as we shall see, they were not yet aware how powerful a God he was, for the exodus had not yet happened. Cain was the traditional ancestor of the Kenites, and the mark of Cain was the mark of Yahweh:

Then Yahweh [the Hebrew word translated throughout the RSV by LORD in capitals] said to him, Not so! If anyone slays Cain, vengeance shall be taken on him sevenfold. And Yahweh put a mark on Cain, lest any who came upon him should kill him. [Gn 4:15]

There are other scraps of evidence scattered through the Old Testament, based on Rechab being a Kenite; the sequence of argument runs: 1 Chr 2:55 (Catholic bibles sometimes call this book 1 Paralipomena), 2 Kgs 10:15–16 (4 Kgs in Catholic bibles), and Jer 35, where they appear as a particularly devout and strict sect of Judaism. Outside the bible there is a particularly impressive Egyptian text dated about 1300 BC which refers to a place near Kenite settlements as YHW, and this is all the more striking for being near the most probable of the dates given to Moses.

But it is the event after the exodus which really carries the weight, and although this is to anticipate the sequence of events, it will perhaps be more helpful to deal with it now.

According to Exodus, the people moved down the western coast of the Sinai Peninsula to the area where Egypt mined turquoise and copper, until they came to Rephidim at the foot of Mount Sinai. At this point Jethro appeared again. The Midianites were nomads, moving their flocks to wherever pasturage was to be found, so this need not be the same area as the incident when Moses first met Jethro before the exodus. Jethro came because he had heard rumour of the Hebrew escape from Egypt:

> Jethro, the priest of Midian, Moses' father-in-law, heard of all that God had done for Moses and for Israel his people, how the Lord had brought Israel out of Egypt ... Then Moses told his father-in-law all that the Lord had done to Pharaoh and to the Egyptians for Israel's sake, all the hardship that had come upon them in the way, and how the Lord had delivered them. [Ex 18:1, 8]

So far there is nothing exceptional. It is in the next few verses that the vital statement occurs:

> And Jethro rejoiced for all the good which the Lord had done to Israel, in that he had delivered them out of the hand of the Egyptians. And Jethro said, Blessed be the Lord, who has delivered you out of the hand of the Egyptians and out of the hand of Pharaoh. Now I know that the Lord is greater than all gods, because he has delivered the people from under the hand of the Egyptians, when they dealt arrogantly with them. [Gn 18:9–11]

The really important phrase is, 'Now I know that the Lord is greater than all gods'. This could mean that up till then Jethro had worshipped some other god but he now switched his allegiance to Yahweh. But it can also mean that Jethro had worshipped Yahweh all along and that the recent events were new proof of his power. He had not realised that Yahweh was so powerful that he could bring his people out from the might of Egypt and defeat an Egyptian army sent in pursuit of them. The events of the exodus added new dimensions and depths to a faith already there. Hitherto Jethro had been in much the same position as Moses before the exodus, during his stay with him in the desert. Since then Moses had been through the experience of the flight and the crossing of the Red Sea, and his knowledge of the God they both worshipped was by that much extended. Now he had communicated that knowledge to Jethro: the pupil had repaid the debt he owed his master. 'Now I know', says Jethro, 'that the Lord is greater than all gods.'

The next happenings confirm this and make it the only possible explanation. The meeting with Jethro was followed by sacrifice:

And Jethro, Moses' father-in-law, offered a burnt offering and sacrifices to God; and Aaron came with all the elders of Israel to eat bread with Moses' father-in-law before God. [Ex 18: 12]

Jethro presided at the sacrifice. It is inconceivable that Jethro could have done so if he had not been recognised by Moses and the people as a priest of the God whom they worshipped. Nor is it easy to suppose that Jethro could have done this if he had only just accepted Yahweh as his god. As Rowley puts it, 'It is unusual for a novice to preside at his own initiation.'[1] Jethro presided because he was the obvious person to do so, a priest of Yahweh.

The sacrifice was followed by another incident when Jethro had the opportunity of seeing Moses administer justice:

> On the morrow Moses sat to judge the people, and the people stood about Moses from morning till evening. When Moses' father-in-law saw all that he was doing for the people, he said, What is this that you are doing for the people? Why do you sit alone, and all the people stand about you from morning till evening? And Moses said to his father-in-law, Because the people come to me to inquire of God; when they have a dispute, they come to me and I decide between a man and his neighbour, and I make them know the statutes of God and his decisions. [Ex 18:13–16]

This is the ordinary, everyday work of a judge administering the law. What is strange to us is that this is essentially a priestly function. Some six hundred years after the exodus the author of the Book of Deuteronomy, in his collection of law and procedure, emphasised the priestly nature of what we regard as a purely secular office:

[1] *Studies in the Old Testament*, London 1963, 52.

If any case require decision between one kind of homicide and another, one kind of legal right and another, or one kind of assault and another, any case within your towns which is too difficult for you, then you shall arise and go up to the place which the Lord your God will choose, and coming to the Levitical priests, and to the judge who is in office in those days, you shall consult them, and they shall declare to you the decision . . . The man who acts presumptuously, by not obeying the priest who stands to administer there before the Lord your God, or the judge, that man shall die; so you shall purge the evil from Israel. [Dt 17:8–12]

Moses was performing a priestly task when he sat to administer the law, he told the people what God's will was in their particular case. And precisely because it was a priestly work, Jethro felt that he had a right to instruct Moses in his task of interpreting Yahweh's will to his people:

Moses' father-in-law said to him, What you are doing is not good. You and the people with you will wear yourselves out, for the thing is too heavy for you; you are not able to perform it alone. Listen now to my voice; I will give you counsel, and God be with you! . . . [Ex 18:17–19]

And Jethro went on to tell Moses how to organise the administration of justice. If Jethro were not a Yahweh priest this would be an act of great presumption.

This has been a long digression, but it has enabled us to place Moses in an understandable religious context and to penetrate a little further into the mystery surrounding the first revelation made by God to Moses when he was staying with Jethro. The opening verse of chapter 3, where the account of the revelation is given, belongs to the later priestly writings, but the rest is compounded of the two early sources. To a large extent they overlap, and the incident is more clearly seen if we concentrate mainly on the 'J' source again. It says this:

And the angel of the Lord appeared to him in a flame of fire out of the midst of a bush; and he looked, and lo, the bush was burning, yet it was not consumed. And Moses said, I will turn aside and see this great sight, why the bush is not burned. When the Lord saw that he turned aside to see, he said, Do not come near; put off your shoes from your feet, for the place on which you are standing is holy ground. Then the Lord said, I have seen the affliction of my people who are in Egypt, and have heard their cry because of their taskmasters; I know their sufferings, and I have come down to deliver them out of the hand of the Egyptians, and to bring them up out of that land to a good and broad land, a land flowing with milk and honey, to the place of the Canaanites, the Hittites, the Amorites, the Perizzites, the Hivites, and the Jebusites. Go and gather the elders of Israel together, and say to them, The Lord, the God of your fathers, the God of Abraham, of Isaac, and of Jacob, has appeared to me, saying, I have observed you and what has been done to you in Egypt; and I promise that I will bring you up out of the affliction of Egypt, to the land of the Canaanites, the Hittites, the Amorites, the Perizzites, the Hivites, and the Jebusites, a land flowing with milk and honey. And they will hearken to your voice; and you and the elders of Israel shall go to the king of Egypt and say to him, The Lord, the God of the Hebrews, has met with us; and now, we pray you, let us go a three days' journey into the wilderness, that we may sacrifice to the Lord our God. [Ex 3:2–4a, 5, 7–8, 16–18]

Let us clear away some minor points about this account so that they do not get in the way of the main thing. 'The angel of the Lord' is a round-about way of talking about God himself, as is shown by the rest of the passage where it is God who is present and God who speaks. The phenomenon of the unconsumed burning bush need not deter us either. Apart from taking it quite literally, it has also been suggested that it might be explained by static electricity, such as St Elmo's Fire, or just be a bush with an unusually brilliant foliage. The circumstances of the revelation are not the important thing about it: the consequences of it are what matter. The peoples named were all inhabitants of Palestine. Where the names refer to groups covering a larger area than the one that the Israelites in fact occupied, it is to be taken as referring to the members of those larger groups who were living in Palestine. This is particularly true of the Hittites and the Amorites: there is no suggestion that the Israelites were to occupy most of what is now Turkey and a good deal of Mesopotamia.

The really important thing about this revelation is that it is God who is himself doing it all, present and active, himself hearing and knowing and doing. It is a direct assertion of the presence of God amongst his people, active to save them from their hopeless condition:

> I have seen the affliction of my people who are in Egypt, and have heard their cry because of their taskmasters; I know their sufferings, and I have come down to deliver them . . . [Ex 3:7–8]

Moses' place in the scheme is to be the herald, the messenger, the commentator who is to tell the people what is happening. Then he and the elders of the people are to go to Pharaoh as the representatives of God, his ambassadors, and tell Pharaoh what God wants him to do:

> Go and gather the elders of Israel together, and say to them . . . ; and you and the elders of Israel shall go to the king of Egypt and say to him, The Lord, the God of the Hebrews has met with us; and now, we pray you, let us go a three days' journey . . . [Ex 3:16, 18]

All through the events of the exodus this theme runs: it is the power of God that is at work, not in any sense the power or strength of men. This is underlined, in fact, in the other ancient source, by Moses' protest of his own inadequacy:

> But Moses said to God, Who am I that I should go to Pharaoh, and bring the sons of Israel out of Egypt? He (God) said, But I will be with you . . . [Ex 3:11–12]

This is the authentic note of response when God requires his servants to do anything for him, and without it there is no chance of God's power working unhindered. One could give instances of it throughout the bible. St Paul went so far as to say that God deliberately chooses the weak and inadequate to do his work, so that there can be no doubt where the power is coming from:

> But we have this treasure in earthen vessels, to show that the transcendent power belongs to God and not to us. [2 Cor 4:7]

and the rebuke of Peter by Jesus was earned because Peter was thinking in terms of what a man could do and the methods a man might employ (Mk 8:31ff.).

How would Moses convince the people that he really had received a revelation from God, and a revelation, moreover, which involved the people putting themselves in extreme danger and making demands of Pharaoh—even in the mild form of obtaining a week's leave—which he was bound to reject? Fundamentally, the answer to this problem was that they would in fact listen: 'And they will hearken to your voice' (Ex 3:18). For Moses would be speaking with the authority of God himself and that authority would show. It was an authority, moreover, with which they already had some familiarity, for it was the God of their fathers who had appeared to Moses, not a strange new God whose authority had never been accepted amongst them. They did not yet know, any more than Jethro did, how very great his power was: that would not be known until he had shown his power by actually getting them out of Egypt, but they had the precedent of traditions of obedience in their own history. How vague that history was, we do not know; certainly it was far more vague than the Book of Genesis would have us believe, but at least it was something:

> Say to them, The Lord, the God of your fathers, the God of Abraham, of Isaac, and of Jacob, has appeared to me . . . [Ex 3:16]

Later we must go into the question of whether the Hebrews in Egypt in fact worshipped God under the name Yahweh. It seems probable that they did not, and that the name was going to be something new to them, something Moses would tell them. The important thing now is that Moses was speaking to them with the authority of a God whom they could identify, a God with whom they had already had dealings. And if God was to act through Moses in such a vast matter as leading the people out of Egypt, then his power would be convincing when Moses told the people that it was there.

At the same time Moses would tell the people

something of the character of God, and here we must dip into the other ancient source, the one that emerged in the northern kingdom, for that explains the name Yahweh. The explanation is given in answer to Moses' problem of what he answers when the people ask what God's name is:

> Then Moses said to God, If I come to the people of Israel and say to them, The God of your fathers has sent me to you, and they ask me, What is his name? what shall I say to them? God said to Moses, I AM WHO I AM. And he said, Say this to the people of Israel, I AM has sent me to you . . . : this is my name for ever, and thus I am to be remembered throughout all generations. [Ex 3:13-15]

The root of the Hebrew verb 'to be' is HYH, and 'Yahweh' can easily be accepted as a third person singular form of this, in which the middle 'y' has been replaced by 'w' to avoid repetition of the letter. 'Yahweh' would then mean, 'He is'.

'What's in a name?' A great deal. The name of a person, for the ancient Hebrew—and a great many people nowadays, for that matter—was far more than a convenient method of avoiding confusion. Many of us have had the experience of being known mainly as a number, and one sometimes feels that perhaps a name is a sort of number: what does it matter whether one is referred to as PO/RM/AR/GCI/PMX776308, for the Royal Navy's mysterious purposes, or as Joseph Rhymer? The ancient attitude may be seen from

Peter's reply to the people after he had healed the cripple at one of the temple gates:

> Men of Israel, why do you wonder at this, or why do you stare at us, as though by our own power or piety we had made him walk? The God of Abraham and of Isaac and of Jacob, the God of our fathers, glorified his servant Jesus, whom you delivered up and denied in the presence of Pilate, when he had decided to release him. But you denied the Holy and Righteous One, and asked for a murderer to be granted to you, and killed the Author of life, whom God raised from the dead. To this we are witnesses. And his name, by faith in his name, has made this man strong whom you see and know . . . [Ac 3:12–16]

At the subsequent examination of Peter and John by the high priest and his associates, the question was put directly in terms of 'name' as synonymous with 'power': 'By what power or by what name did you do this?' (Ac 4:7). The name expressed the character of the person named, for an ancient; it told you what the person was like; and if the person's character changed radically or he was given a new responsibility, his name might be changed to fit his new position. So, as we have seen, 'Jacob' was changed to 'Israel', and, also, Simon was given the special name Peter by Jesus. If Moses were asked about the character of the God who had spoken to him and given him authority, it would make sense for him to reply, 'His name is Yahweh', or, 'His name is "I am".'

But here we really must be careful, for to us, 'being' is likely to convey a good deal less than it did to the Hebrew. For us it is all too likely to mean 'mere' existence, a static state of just being there, the kind of approach which some of the discussions about 'proofs for the existence of God' adopt. This is emphatically not the approach here. For the Hebrew (and, I believe, for us too) it is impossible to think of 'being' separated from doing, from activity. 'I am' could not possibly be some kind of passive God, present yet inactive. If he exists, and is amongst his people, then you can expect things to happen. More than that, the expansion elaborates the basic revelation:

If . . . they ask me, What is his name? what shall I say to them? God said to Moses, I AM WHO I AM. [Ex 3:13–14]

The phrase 'I am who I am' employs the continuous tense of the Hebrew verb. Hebrew only has two tenses, one to express completed action, and one to express incomplete, or continuous action, and the latter is employed to express the future. So this phrase conveys continuity, activity in the future continuous with action in the past and present. Used of God it implies, as well, consistency and dependability. Within the context of past revelations to Abraham and Isaac and Jacob, and God's activity amongst them, and their response to his active presence, the phrase takes on a great complex of dimensions of meaning:

Then Moses said to God, If I come to the

people of Israel and say to them, the God of your fathers has sent me to you, and they ask me, what is his name? what shall I say to them? God said to Moses, I AM WHO I AM (continually, eternally, actively). And he said, Say this to the people of Israel, I AM has sent me to you. God also said to Moses, Say this to the people of Israel, The Lord, the God of your fathers, the God of Abraham, the God of Isaac, and the God of Jacob, has sent me to you: this is my name for ever, and thus I am to be remembered throughout all generations. [Ex 3: 13–15]

Later in her history, under the prophets, Israel explored the meaning of this statement of power, and saw that God's dependability went far beyond any human concept of a mere contractual relationship. Hosea discovered something about it through the breakdown of his marriage, and discovered that Yahweh's love for his people endured any insult they might pay him. The anonymous prophet of the exile, as we might expect, illuminated it:

Can a woman forget her sucking child,
    that she should have no compassion on the
    son of her womb?
Even these may forget,
    yet I will not forget you.
Behold, I have graven you on the palms of my
    hands. [Is 49:15–16]

The text continues, in chapter 4, with three

miraculous signs given to Moses to prove his power and authority to the people; a rod which turned to a snake when dropped and back to a rod when picked up again, the ability to make his hand leprous or unmarked at will, and the ability to turn water into blood. But he in fact never used these signs, and one suspects that they found their way in as the kind of powers a messenger of God might be expected to have. What is more important is the place assigned to Aaron. Moses protested to God, according to the Yahwist source, that he was unable to speak convincingly, and received the answer one might expect, an answer similar to the one Jeremiah received when he pleaded that he did not know how to speak:

> But Moses said to the Lord, Oh, my Lord, I am not eloquent, either heretofore or since thou hast spoken to thy servant; but I am slow of speech and of tongue. Then the Lord said to him, Who has made man's mouth? Who makes him dumb, or deaf, or seeing, or blind? Is it not I, the Lord? Now therefore go, and I will be with your mouth and teach you what you shall speak. [Ex 4:10–12]

Surprisingly, Moses did not accept this reassurance, but went further and asked to be excused from the whole business. Angrily, God appointed Aaron to be Moses' spokesman, to speak the words which Moses tells him to speak, and Moses, of course, would get the words from God:

> But he said, Oh, my Lord, send, I pray, some other person. Then the anger of the Lord was

kindled against Moses and he said, Is there not Aaron, your brother, the Levite? I know that he can speak well; and behold, he is coming out to meet you, and when he sees you he will be glad in his heart. And you shall speak to him and put the words in his mouth; and I will be with your mouth and with his mouth, and will teach you what you shall do. He shall speak for you to the people; and he shall be a mouth for you, and you shall be to him as God. [Ex 4: 13–16]

It is a remarkable passage and one cannot help but be suspicious of it, particularly as the same source, the 'J' tradition, depicts Moses speaking effectively to Pharaoh a number of times without the aid of Aaron. In other traditions, particularly the priestly one, Aaron's position is made very important. Aaron wields the rod and uses it to outdo Pharaoh's magicians and bring about the miracles of the plagues. The answer is to be seen, probably, in the later development of the priesthood amongst the Israelites. Like other functions, such as the kingship, the priesthood was not a matter of vocation but of inheritance. A man could only be considered for the priesthood if he were the son of a priest, unless he had physical defects which rendered him ineligible in any case. Consequently the priests were interrelated, and together constituted the tribe of Levi, or, to be more accurate, were part of the tribe of Levi, for the Levites comprised everyone concerned with the administration of the temple and of the sacrifices. The temple police, for example, would be Levites. Within the tribe of Levi, only certain families were entitled to perform the sacrifices themselves, and all of these traced their descent back to Aaron, Moses' brother. Can one see the influence of this in the position ascribed to Aaron in the accounts of the exodus? Certainly there were many people, and those the very ones responsible for the transmission of the traditions, who were concerned that Aaron should be seen as someone with important responsibilities, and the accounts become far more credible if one recognises this influence at work.

The complex revelation ends with the warning that Pharaoh would resist Moses' demands:

> When you go back to Egypt, see that you do before Pharaoh all the miracles which I have put in your power; but I will harden his heart, so that he will not let the people go. [Ex 4:21]

This too belongs to the oldest source, and it is interesting to see how extensive it recognises God's power to be. It is understandable that it should assume that God has the power to do whatever he wants in Egypt, but this goes beyond that idea. It rests on the assumption that everything that happens is done by God, even when the agent is Pharaoh. So when Pharaoh refused to let the Israelites go, it was because God had made him refuse. This is very difficult for us to accept, for it makes the morality of Pharaoh's acts very obscure: how can Pharaoh be blamed if he is not responsible? It is worth noticing, however, that the Hebrew narrator sees a reason in this: it is to give the opportunity for God to show how strong he is. For God to demonstrate his strength there must be opposition, otherwise the extent of his strength would never be known. Halfway through the plagues, where the hardening of Pharaoh's heart is frequently mentioned, there is an explanatory addition:

> Then the Lord said to Moses, Go in to Pharaoh; for I have hardened his heart and the heart of his servants, that I may show these signs of mine among them, and that you may tell in the hearing of your son and of your son's son how I have made sport of the Egyptians and what signs I have done among them; that you may know that I am the Lord. [Ex 10:1–2]

This is a theme which St Paul took up in Romans, when he was writing about the universality of God's power and of his control of history:

> For the scripture says to Pharaoh, I have raised you up for the very purpose of showing my power in you, so that my name may be proclaimed in all the earth. [Rm 9:17]

Pharaoh may think he is in control of events, but he is in the presence of a power infinitely greater than his, in whose hands he is no more than a tool. It is out of this kind of thinking that full monotheism develops.

Moses returned to Egypt, and called the elders together:

And the people believed; and when they heard that the Lord had visited the people of Israel and that he had seen their affliction, they bowed their heads and worshipped. [Ex 4:31]

Additional Notes

The Old Testament

The 'J' source, from the opening of the Book of Exodus to the beginning of the plagues, is to be found in the following passages:

Ex 1:6, 8–12, 14b, 20b; 2:11–23; 3:2–4a, 5, 7–8, 16–18; 4:1–16, 19–20, 21–26, 29–31.

The accounts of the call of Moses and the covenant made with him and the people are to be found in Ex 3:6–15; 6:2–8.

Moses' reaction to his call by God and the responsibility laid upon him can be paralleled in:

Is 6:5–7
Jer 1:6–10
Ezek 2:6–7

The New Testament

Lk 5:8 (the call of Peter)
Ac 26:15–18
2 Cor 4:7–15; 11:16 – 12:10 (Paul's accounts of his call, and of his experience in responding to it).

You might like to consider: what work God calls men to do for him in our own society and times; and what qualities he looks for in those whom he calls.

4

The escape

An enormous amount of work has been done during the past hundred years on the problem of separating and recognising the different strands of tradition used in the account of the exodus. In this chapter we shall be concerned with the plagues, the Passover, and the crossing of the 'Red Sea'. We shall find that by continuing to concentrate, in the main, on one strand of the tradition, the extremely complicated sequence of events will be much easier to follow. The strand we are using is the 'Yahwist' tradition, the earliest to reach a settled form, and the most complete of the traditions used in the first few books of the bible.

The account of the plagues by which Pharaoh and the Egyptians were progressively 'softened up' until, in the end, they not only gave the Israelites leave to go but drove them out, occupies chapters 7 to 12 of Exodus. The three main strands are woven together very closely throughout, but each has preserved characteristic differences. In the earliest tradition Moses' role is entirely that of a messenger whose job it is to tell Pharaoh what God wants and what he will do if Pharaoh does not obey. This can be seen clearly if we take this

'J', or 'Yahwist' strand in the account of the first plague:

> Then the Lord said to Moses, Pharaoh's heart is hardened, he refuses to let the people go. Go to Pharaoh in the morning, as he is going out to the water; wait for him by the river's brink, and you shall say to him, The Lord, the God of the Hebrews, sent me to you, saying, Let my people go, that they may serve me in the wilderness; and, behold, you have not yet obeyed. Thus says the Lord, By this you shall know that I am the Lord: behold, I will strike the water that is in the Nile, and it shall be turned to blood, and the fish in the Nile shall die, and the Nile shall become foul, and the Egyptians will loathe to drink water from the Nile. And all the water that was in the Nile turned to blood. And the fish in the Nile died; and the Nile became foul, so that the Egyptians could not drink water from the Nile. And all the Egyptians dug round about the Nile for water to drink, for they could not drink the water of the Nile. [Ex 7:14–15a, 16–18 except the middle of 17, 20b–21a, 24]

Within the same passage, the slightly later 'E' tradition makes Moses bring about the plague, at God's command of course, by striking the surface of the water with his rod. At the meeting with Pharaoh, this tradition adds 'and take in your hand the rod which was turned into a serpent' (Ex 7:15b), and just before the river changes colour it adds 'in the sight of Pharaoh and in the sight of his servants, he lifted up the rod and

97

struck the water that was in the Nile' (Ex 7:20, middle).

The priestly tradition, written during the years just after the first groups returned from the period of exile in Babylon, some two hundred and fifty or three hundred years after the 'E' tradition reached fixed form, goes further still. Just as Moses is God's agent, so Aaron appears as Moses' agent and a 'chain of command' is formed:

> And the Lord said to Moses, Say to Aaron, Take your rod and stretch out your hand over the waters of Egypt, over their rivers, their canals, and their ponds, and all their pools of water, that they may become blood; and there shall be blood throughout all the land of Egypt, both in vessels of wood and in vessels of stone. Moses and Aaron did as the Lord commanded, and the blood was throughout all the land of Egypt. [Ex 7:19–20a, 21b]

By this time, in the development of the story, not only the Nile but every drop of water in Egypt has turned to blood. There are historical reasons for this heightening of Aaron's position, as we have seen, particularly when we remember that this part of the tradition evolved amongst the small group struggling to rebuild Jerusalem after it had lain in ruins for half a century. They badly needed reassurance, particularly the reassurance that the priests who were leading them had the authority to do so. They were surrounded by opposition and difficulty, both from the neighbouring non-Israelites and from a rival group of Hebrew priests who had managed to avoid being involved in the exile. They found their support in the reassurance that Aaron, their ancestor, had been Moses' lieutenant at the exodus and his spokesman. It gives us an indication of how central the exodus was to their faith, but it does not help us very much in the task of finding what actually happened in Egypt during the time of Moses.

If we make a list of the plagues and the traditions which mention them, we find that some are mentioned in more than one of the traditions while others are only to be found in one of them. The results are these:

1. The Nile water turns the colour of blood and becomes undrinkable (Ex 7:14–24): found in J, E, and P.
2. Swarms of frogs (Ex 7:25 – 8:15): found in J and P.
3. Gnats or mosquitoes (Ex 8:16–19): P only.
4. Flies (Ex 8:20–32): J only.
5. A cattle plague (Ex 9:1–7): J only.
6. Boils and sores on men and cattle (Ex 9:8–12): P only.
7. Hail (Ex 9:13–35): found in J and E.
8. Locusts (Ex 10:1–20): found in J and E.
9. Darkness for three days (Ex 10:21–23): E only.
10. Death of the first-born (Ex 11:1–12:34): J, E, and P.

In this list it can be seen that two of the plagues mentioned by the priestly tradition alone are very similar to two neighbouring plagues mentioned by the earlier 'J' tradition: gnats or mosquitoes, and flies; and the cattle plague, and boils and sores affecting both men and cattle. In each case it is safe to assume that there has been duplication.

This reduces the plagues to eight, and with the exception of the final one, they are all misfortunes which were fairly common occurrences in Egypt and which can be accounted for naturally over the course of a few months. In fact, with some of them, if one is so minded, a causal sequence is possible. The reddening of the Nile waters is an annual feature as mineral deposits are washed into the upper waters of the Nile by the summer rains in the mountains of Ethiopia (it must be remembered that there are no substantial tributaries running into the Nile for the lower thousand miles of its course). This time, unusually, the waters were polluted to the point where they were unfit to drink, and the fish died. There is no need to accept the priestly source's development of this to the point where all water in the country, whether in the river or not, was contaminated, in fact the digging of wells round the river, so that the soil acted as a filter for the water, tells against this.

Frogs were driven from the river; mosquitoes and flies are a common condition and may have bred in unusual numbers if the river was polluted, and this could have led to an outbreak of disease. Hail and locusts are recurring phenomena, and the three-day darkness (which is only found in one source, although it is one of the two older ones) has been connected with the terrible sand-storms which sweep in from the desert. In each case the miraculous element lies not in the occurrence itself, but in the timing of it and the way Moses coupled it with Israel's need. As the series of plagues are set out in the narrative, they are coupled with a progressive weakening by Pharaoh in the stand he had taken against letting the people go to sacrifice. It begins with not only a flat refusal but with orders that the Hebrews' burdens were to be increased (Ex 5:3–21) to the point where the people complained to Moses that his interference had only increased their misery. Pharaoh then gave permission for the Hebrews to hold their sacrifice in Egypt, but this Moses refused because some of the animals they sacrificed were sacred to the Egyptians, and to sacrifice them would provoke a riot. The only answer was to go out into the desert, well away from Egyptians and their territory:

> Then Pharaoh called Moses and Aaron, and said, Go, sacrifice to your God within the land. But Moses said, it would not be right to do so; for we shall sacrifice to the Lord our God offerings abominable to the Egyptians. If we sacrifice offerings abominable to the Egyptians before their eyes, will they not stone us? We must go three days' journey into the wilderness and sacrifice to the Lord our God as he will command us. [Ex 8:25–27 ('J').]

Later (Ex 10:11) permission was given for the adult males to go alone, and then (Ex 10:24) for all the people to go provided they left their cattle and sheep behind. All this Moses refused, until he was dismissed by Pharaoh in anger and told not to reappear. 'Moses said, As you say! I will not see your face again' (Ex 10:29). The final plague was to be the death of the Egyptian firstborn.

What lies behind the tradition of the death of the Egyptian firstborn it is now impossible to say. In the source we have been using the effect is depicted as extending throughout Egypt:

> And Moses said, Thus says the Lord, About midnight I will go forth in the midst of Egypt; and all the first-born in the land of Egypt shall die, from the first-born of Pharaoh who sits upon his throne, even to the first-born of the maidservant who is behind the mill; and all the first-born of the cattle. And there shall be a great cry throughout all the land of Egypt, such as there has never been, nor ever shall be again. But against any of the people of Israel, either man or beast, not a dog shall growl; that you may know that the Lord makes a distinction between the Egyptians and Israel. [Ex 11:4–7]

And so it happened (Ex 12:29–34), and the Egyptians urged the Israelites to leave. What is important is that the traditions make this the occasion for giving the origins of the Passover, and of two other religious rites.

In fact, the Passover shows all the signs of being a good deal older even than the exodus. In the Book of Exodus the information about the Passover is given in three sections: Ex 12:1–14 (P); Ex 12:21–27 (J); and Ex 12:43–50 (P). There is some repetition between the two traditions, but on the whole they are complementary; the second 'P' section (12:43–50) deals with the admission of non-Israelites to the rite.

Firstly, this was a family sacrifice in which no priest was needed. The head of the family presided at it and performed the actual sacrifice together with the other heads of families:

> Tell all the congregation of Israel that on the tenth day of this month they shall take every man a lamb according to their fathers' houses, a lamb for a household; and if the household is too small for a lamb, then a man and his neighbour next to his house shall take according to the number of persons: according to what each can eat you shall take your count for the lamb. Your lamb shall be without blemish, a male a year old; you shall take it from the sheep or from the goats; and you shall keep it until the fourteenth day of this month, when the whole assembly of the congregation of Israel shall kill their lambs in the evening. [Ex 12:3–6]

As in any other communion sacrifice, the blood was then poured out. In the Passover sacrifice, the blood was used in a special way:

> Take a bunch of hyssop and dip it in the blood which is in the basin, and touch the lintel and the two doorposts with the blood which is in the basin; and none of you shall go out of the door of his house until the morning. [Ex 12:22]

The lamb was then roasted and eaten with unrisen bread and wild herbs, and any part of it which was uneaten was burned:

They shall eat the flesh that night, roasted; with unleavened bread and bitter herbs they shall eat it. Do not eat any of it raw or boiled with water, but roasted, its head with its legs and its inner parts. And you shall let none of it remain until the morning, anything that remains until the morning you shall burn. [Ex 12:8–10]

Finally, the whole sacrifice and meal were to be done in a hurry with everyone dressed for journeying:

In this manner you shall eat it: your loins girded, your sandals on your feet, and your staff in your hand; and you shall eat it in haste. It is the Lord's passover. [Ex 12:11]

This rite shows all the signs of belonging to the way of life of a nomad shepherd community living by driving their flocks from pasture to pasture. It provides for circumstances in which there is no need to use utensils: the dough does not have to be left to rise, it can be baked straight on a hot stone, and the lamb is roasted so that no pan is needed. The seasoning is the kind of herb which can be found growing in the desert, and the bread is the same kind of bread as the nomadic Bedouin Arabs still use today. De Vaux sums it up:

It may have been a feast celebrated when the tribe struck camp before setting out for the spring pastures, but this is not the whole explanation: it was, in a more general way, an offering for the welfare of the flock, like the old

Arab feast which fell in the month of Rajab, the first month of spring.[1]

And this is where the significance of the use of the blood would lie. For in Hebrew thought, blood was important because it contained the life of the animal:

> For the life of the flesh is in the blood; and I have given it you upon the altar to make atonement for your souls; for it is the blood that makes atonement, by reason of the life. [Lv 17: 11]

The blood contained the life of the victim, and was filled with the divine power both because all life came from God, and also because the victim was a gift given to God and therefore belonging to him. The blood of the lamb was used to overcome any evil power which might threaten the tribe or its flocks, and it was smeared on the tentpoles to ward the evil away. There is a very strong hint of this in the earlier account of the Passover, the 'J' tradition, where there is a reference to a 'destroyer' active during the night:

> For the Lord will pass through to slay the Egyptians; and when he sees the blood on the lintel and on the two doorposts, the Lord will pass over the door, and will not allow the destroyer to enter your houses to slay you. [Ex 12:23]

There is no sign of any worry about God himself

[1] *Ancient Israel*, London 1961, 489.

doing the killing in the rest of the account of the exodus, and it is hard to see why a 'destroyer' should be introduced here, but it does make sense if part of the purpose of the Passover rite, before its connection with the exodus, was to protect men and flocks against evil powers.

We have used the phrase, 'before its connection with the exodus'. We shall have more to say about this later, when we look at the relationship between the exodus events and the whole life of the people in later years. Meanwhile, it is worth saying this. The death of the Egyptian first-born is surrounded by obscurity. It is, of course, possible that the traditions are literally accurate and every Egyptian family lost its eldest child and all the earliest of its calves and lambs:

> At midnight the Lord smote all the first-born in the land of Egypt, from the first-born of Pharaoh who sat on his throne to the first-born of the captive who was in the dungeon, and all the first-born of the cattle. And Pharaoh rose up in the night, he, and all his servants; and there was a great cry in Egypt, for there was not a house where one was not dead. [Ex 12:29–30]

and the Israelites suffered no loss at all. But there are other possibilities. One is that there was a death just in the royal household at the time of the exodus, and the account expanded this to cover all of the Egyptians. The other possibility is far more radical. It is the view that the Passover became associated with the exodus because the escape from Egypt took place at the same time of year as the Passover sacrifice, and that the Passover rite influenced the traditions about what happened when the people left Egypt. This is the exact reverse, in fact, of the way the Book of Exodus puts it, where the Passover arose out of the events of the exodus, but it is an attractive view-point despite this.

As we have seen, the Passover looks very much like an ancient nomadic shepherd sacrifice which the Israelites had practised before the exodus and even, possibly, before their entry into Egypt when they were nomadic tribes working through northern Arabia and Palestine. The traditions say that there was a sacrifice which the people wanted to make—and a sacrifice, moreover, which had as its object the averting of misfortune—and this was why the people wanted to go out into the desert from Egypt:

> And they said (to Pharaoh), The God of the Hebrews has met with us; Let us go, we pray, a three days' journey into the wilderness, and sacrifice to the Lord our God, lest he fall upon us with pestilence or with the sword. [Ex 5:3]

This is the same 'J' tradition, the earliest we have, which introduces the idea of a destroyer into the account of the Passover. So it is at least probable that the Israelites, with their shepherd traditions, wanted to celebrate the Passover. They then escaped from Egypt at the time of year when they had the Passover sacrifice, and the Passover became the appropriate commemoration of the exodus—whatever it might have been before. There is even a hint of this in the account of the Passover, first in Ex 12:11, where it says 'It is the Lord's passover' as if it were already something the people knew about, and again a little later where 'this day' could mean a day which was already a special day and which was now to become a memorial of the exodus:

> This day shall be for you a memorial day, and you shall keep it as a feast to the Lord; throughout your generations you shall observe it as an ordinance for ever. [Ex 12:14]

If this is so, then the Passover ritual could have influenced the account of what happened in Egypt before the people escaped. The Passover contains a ritual for using blood to avert evil, and it is possible that the death of the first-born entered the traditions as a result of this blood ritual, as an answer to the question, 'What form did this evil take which the Passover sacrifice kept away from the Israelites?' Certainly, the whole account of the exodus reached its present form as part of the rite of the Passover, when the children asked their fathers why they kept the feast and were told the exodus story.

It is worth noticing at this point—and this, too, is something to which we shall have to return—that two other religious observances of later Israel were attached to the exodus and given explanations rooted in the events of the exodus. One was the feast of Unleavened Bread, which is described in Ex 12:14–20 and 13:3–10 (it should be noted that this is *not* the same as the Passover: it became attached to the Passover at a later stage, as we shall see), and the other is the rite of the Dedication of the First-Born, which is given in Ex 13: 11–16. For each of these, Passover, Unleavened Bread, and Dedication of the First-Born, provision is made that the children should be given an explanation in terms of the escape from Egypt. Here again, these provisions all belong to the oldest source, the 'J' tradition:

> And when your children say to you, What do you mean by this service? you shall say, It is the sacrifice of the Lord's passover, for he passed over the houses of the people of Israel in Egypt, when he slew the Egyptians but spared our houses. [Ex 12:27]

(It is worth saying at once that this explanation of the meaning of the word 'passover' is a very strained one, and the root verb 'pasah' is found nowhere else used with this meaning.) Then the feast of Unleavened Bread is given a similar origin:

> And you shall tell your son on that day, It is because of what the Lord did for me when I came out of Egypt. [Ex 13:8]

and so, also, the Dedication of the First-Born:

> And when in time to come your son asks you, What does this mean? you shall say to him, By strength of hand the Lord brought us out of Egypt, from the house of bondage. For when Pharaoh stubbornly refused to let us go, the

Lord slew all the first-born in the land of Egypt, both the first-born of man and the first-born of cattle. Therefore I sacrifice to the Lord all the males that first open the womb; but all the first-born of my sons I redeem. [Ex 13:14–15]

'Redeem' means, in this case, purchase by substituting an animal sacrifice.

Does this shock us—that the information we have about the exodus may have been influenced, or even formed, by the rites which became associated with it? That far from the rites being accurate commemorations, re-presentations, re-enactments of events which occurred during the exodus, it is possible that the reports of the events were formed to fit in with the rites? At first sight of course it shocks us, and we feel that the ground is shaking under our feet. If Judaism is a historical religion, a faith grounded on solid historical events, what remains of it if we hack pieces away from the accounts of the main event itself? At first sight, yes. But on reflection, emphatically no. Whatever it was that happened at the exodus, it made such an overwhelming impression on the people who were involved in it that it became the centre of their whole experience. Everything they had ever believed, every part of their religious experience, every fragment of the common culture into which they were born and which transmitted to them the experiences of their ancestors, became centred on this event. All the diverse threads of their lives were organised into one pattern, all the pieces of their lives were rearranged round the exodus. And not only did this happen for the people who took part in it, it also happened for their descendants down through the years. Prophets, teaching about the character of the God whom the nation worshipped, drew their information from the exodus event; lawyers, revising the law and trying to draw the people back from the degradation of vicious foreign cults, wrote the law as if it had been enacted at the time of the exodus; and all through the national life the systematic round of sacrifices sought to enter again the moment of supreme power when God, with a high hand and outstretched arm, brought his people out of Egypt. Far from undermining our confidence that the exodus was a historical fact, the very extent of its influence and of the institutions which it attracted to itself is its strongest evidence.

The people left Egypt, at the time of the Passover, and either because they had fled without his permission, or because he changed his mind, the Pharaoh decided to stop them:

When the king of Egypt was told that the people had fled, the mind of Pharaoh and his servants was changed towards the people, and they said, What is this we have done, that we have let Israel go from serving us? So he made ready his chariot and took his army with him, and took six hundred picked chariots and all the other chariots of Egypt with officers over all of them. And the Lord hardened the heart of Pharaoh king of Egypt and he pursued the

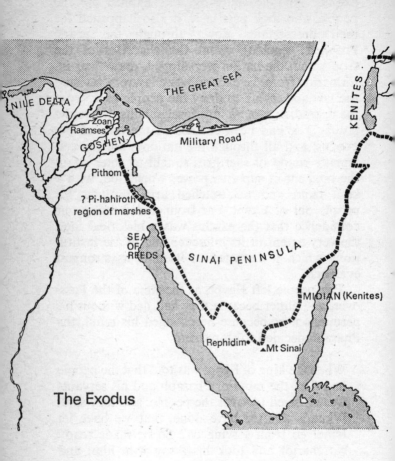

The Exodus

people of Israel as they went forth defiantly. The Egyptians pursued them, all Pharaoh's horses and chariots and his horsemen and his army, and overtook them encamped by the sea, by Pi-ha-hiroth, in front of Baal-zephon. [Ex 14: 5–9]

Unfortunately, although the bible gives plenty of names of places it is no longer possible to identify them, and the strands of tradition which are most confident about the places through which the Hebrews passed are also the ones furthest removed in time from the event. Two encouraging scraps can, however, be salvaged. One is that the name Pi-ha-hiroth probably means 'house of the marshes', and the other is that the phrase *yam-suf* in Ex 13:18, 15:4 and 15:22, the vital references, does *not* mean 'Red Sea' (as our English translations give) but 'Sea of Reeds', and the new English version of the Bible entitled *The Jerusalem Bible* (after the French *Bible de Jérusalem* on which it is based) uses this form of words. The northern end of the Gulf of Suez petered out, in ancient times, in marshes covered with the papyrus reed and in the string of shallow lakes. Hebrew uses the same word, yam, for sea, lake, shore, and even on occasion for such large rivers as the Nile or the Euphrates. With this in mind, the old 'J' tradition begins to give a recognisable picture of what happened. Accompanied by the 'pillar of cloud' and 'pillar of fire' (and we have no idea what they were, except that the tradition sees them as the signs of God's presence), the people got as far as the region of marshes at the northern end of the Gulf of Suez, and there they were held up by the marshes and overtaken by pursuing Egyptian troops:

When Pharaoh drew near, the people of Israel lifted up their eyes, and behold, the Egyptians were marching after them; and they were in great fear. And they said to Moses, Is it because there are no graves in Egypt that you have taken us away to die in the wilderness? What have you done to us, in bringing us out of Egypt? Is not this what we said to you in Egypt, Let us alone and let us serve the Egyptians? For it would have been better for us to serve the Egyptians than to die in the wilderness. And Moses said to the people. Fear not, stand firm, and see the salvation of the Lord, which he will work for you today; for the Egyptians whom you see today, you shall never see again. The Lord will fight for you, and you have only to be still.

And the pillar of cloud moved from before them and stood behind them; and the cloud remained dark on this night (using Noth's translation), and the night passed without one coming near the other. And the Lord drove the sea back by a strong east wind all night, and made the sea dry land. And in the morning watch the Lord in the pillar of fire and of cloud looked down upon the host of the Egyptians, and discomfited the host of the Egyptians, clogging their chariot wheels so that they drove heavily; and the Egyptians said, Let us flee from before Israel; for the Lord fights for them against the Egyptians. And the sea returned to its wonted flow when the morning appeared, and the Egyptians fled into it, and the Lord routed (literally, 'shook off') the Egyptians in the midst of the sea. Thus the Lord saved Israel that day from the hand of the Egyptians; and Israel saw the Egyptians dead upon the sea-shore. [Ex 14:10a, 11–14. 19b, 20b, 21b, 24–25, 27b, 30]

Again, 'seashore' here is literally 'the lip of the sea' and 'lip' is used for any edge: whether of sea, lake, river, marsh or even, of course, the edge of the mouth.

It is still far from possible to be certain, but a reasonable conjecture may be made. Under Moses' leadership and urging, the Israelites moved off into the marshy area helped by a slackening in the flow of water through the watercourses where the wind checked the outfall from the shallow lakes. When the Egyptians attempted to follow them their chariots bogged down in the soft ground, and the dropping of the wind allowed the pent-up water to flow again. If the men in the chariots were armoured—at least with breastplate, helmet and shield, apart from their weapons— they could easily be trapped in the boggy ground and drowned.

However it happened, the people were free from Egypt. The man Moses had come to them with the news that God had spoken to him in the desert, the same God whom their ancestors had worshipped and the God whom they worshipped in their annual sacrifice of a lamb. God had told him that he would lead the people out of Egypt, and they had safely escaped. The proof had been given. They were God's people, the people of a God who was stronger than Egypt. One of the very oldest fragments of poetry in the Old Testament catches the moment:

> Sing to the Lord, for he has triumphed gloriously;
> the horse and his rider he has thrown into the sea. [Ex 15:21]

Additional Notes

The Old Testament

The 'J' source, from the beginning of the plagues to the crossing of the 'Red Sea', is to be found in the following passages:

Ex 5:3 – 6:1; 7:14–15, 16–18 (except 'with the rod that is in my hand'), 20b–21a, 24–25; 8:1–4, 8–15, 20–32; 9:1–7, 13–21, 23b, 24b–30, 32–34; 10:1–11, 13b, 14b–15a, 15c–19, 24–26, 28–29; 11:4–8; 12:29–34, 37–39; 13:3–16, 21–22; 14:5–7, 10a (to 'fear'), 11–14, 19b, 30.

The accounts of the Passover are given in Ex 12:1–14 (P), 21–27 (J), 43–50 (P: conditions for admission of strangers).

The New Testament

There are references to the Passover, with Christ seen as the Passover lamb, in:

Jn 1:29; 19:36
1 Cor 5:7
Heb 9:14
1 Pt 1:19

There are also hints, which would be clear to people familiar with the Passover. For instance, Ex 12:11 finds echoes in Lk 12:35; Eph 6:12 and 1 Pt 1:13.

You might like to consider: whether the popular image of God is a hindrance to the work of God today; and how people think the power of God is shown and made available to them.

5

The covenant

Led by Moses, the people set out down the eastern
shore of the Gulf of Suez. Their journey was
marked by difficulties about water and food, the
constant problems of the nomad, and the three
incidents recounted can all be matched with
natural occurrences which can still be observed.
The brackish water was made palatable by adding a local shrub to it, and the food problem was
overcome by the fortuitous arrival of quails and
the discovery of something edible which they had
never seen before: 'a fine, flake-like thing, fine as
hoar-frost on the ground' (Ex 16:14). Quails pass
the Sinai Peninsula in their spring and summer
migrations, and rest, exhausted and easy to catch.
Noth comments about the 'manna' (a name which
the bible derives from the Hebrew question, 'What
is it?': *man-hu*): 'There is still manna today in the
inland region of the Sinai peninsula, and it is even
called *mann* by the nomadic inhabitants of this
region. It is a sort of drop-like formation on the
leaves of the tree or shrub, native to the wilderness, of the tamarisk, in particular the "manna-
tamarisk", formed of the secretions produced by
the sting of a tree louse. It falls from the leaves
onto the ground and it can be picked up after it

has grown relatively hard in the cool of the night. As it has a low melting temperature it dissolves in the heat of the day and so is best gathered in the early morning. It has a sweet taste and is still a favourite food of the inhabitants of that particular part of the barren desert-land.'[1] This must be the basis of the account in the Book of Exodus:

> Then the Lord said to Moses, Behold, I will rain bread from heaven for you; and the people shall go out and gather a day's portion every day, that I may prove them, whether they will walk in my law or not. On the sixth day, when they prepare what they bring in, it will be twice as much as they gather daily. In the morning dew lay round about the camp. And when the dew had gone up, there was on the face of the wilderness a fine, flake-like thing, fine as hoar-frost on the ground. When the people of Israel saw it, they said to one another, What is it? for they did not know what it was. And Moses said to them, It is the bread which the Lord has given you to eat. [Ex 16:4–5, 13b–15 ('J').]

The element of 'proving' is concerned with the observance of the sabbath.

The complaints of the people against Moses have the ring of hard fact about them, and the theme is repeated throughout the accounts of the journeyings in the desert. The attack by local tribesmen fits in with similar incidents at other periods, particularly when the use of the precious waterholes was involved. The nomad life depicted

[1] *Exodus*, S.C.M. Press 1962, 132.

in the Book of Genesis has a number of incidents where wells and water are the cause of bloodshed. Chapter 18 contains the report of the arrival of Jethro, Moses' father-in-law, and this we have already discussed at length early in chapter 4. It was a fitting moment for Jethro to appear again, as we can now see, for Moses and the people were about to arrive at the holy mountain where their God, Yahweh, would confirm his choice of them and seal the relationship he had revealed by bringing them out of Egypt. As we have seen, Jethro was himself a priest of Yahweh, but without the knowledge of how powerful his God was. That knowledge was now given to him in the account of the people's escape from Egypt, and his reaction expresses the effect the event had had on the Israelites:

> And Jethro said, Blessed be the Lord, who has delivered you out of the hand of the Egyptians and out of the hand of Pharaoh. Now I know that the Lord is greater than all gods, because he delivered the people from under the hand of the Egyptians, when they dealt arrogantly with them. [Ex 18:10–11]

Finally, they all reached the holy mountain, called Sinai in some parts of the tradition and Horeb in others.

There is some doubt as to the exact location of the mountain, but the doubts seem to be based mainly on the view that the mountain has to be volcanic because the description of what happened, in Ex 19, is of a volcanic eruption. This is by no means convincing, for all the phenomena are consistent with a heavy thunderstorm, and there is no mention of ash. It is argued that as there is no volcano in the Sinai peninsula the holy mountain cannot be located there, but if the events are not volcanic this objection fails, and the Sinai peninsula fits in with such places as can be identified in the accounts we have.

The events at the holy mountain are described from chapter 19 onwards in Exodus. Chapter 19 itself is a thorough mixture of different traditions and editorial additions, as we might expect from a section so central to the Hebrew faith, and the only thing we can do is to take it as it comes. It opens with the arrival of the people at the foot of the mountain:

> On the third new moon after the people of Israel had gone forth out of the land of Egypt, on that day they came into the wilderness of Sinai. And when they set out from Rephidim and came into the wilderness of Sinai, they encamped in the wilderness; and there Israel encamped before the mountain. [Ex 19:1-2]

Moses then went up the mountain and God told him to explain to the people that the escape from Egypt was the proof of his power and of his concern for them. They are to become a 'kingdom of priests':

> And Moses went up to God, and the Lord called to him out of the mountain, saying, Thus you shall say to the house of Jacob, and tell the

people of Israel: You have seen what I did to the Egyptians, and how I bore you on eagles' wings and brought you to myself. Now, therefore, if you will obey my voice and keep my covenant, you shall be my own possession among all peoples; for all the earth is mine, and you shall be to me a kingdom of priests and a holy nation. These are the words which you shall speak to the children of Israel. [Ex 19:3–6]

The heart of the matter is there: the confirmation of the promises and the expansion of them beyond anything that had been said in previous covenant statements. The elders of the people, the heads of families, were then told what God had said, followed by the statement that God would speak in the hearing of the whole people, so that their faith could rest on direct experience:

So Moses went and called the elders of the people, and set before them all these words which the Lord had commanded him. And all the people answered together and said, All that the Lord has commanded we will do. And Moses reported the words of the people to the Lord. And the Lord said to Moses, Lo, I am coming to you in a thick cloud, that the people may hear when I speak with you, and may also believe you for ever. [Ex 19:7–9]

There follows a description of the people's preparation for their meeting with God, the warning that no one was to go near the mountain, and that they were to be ritually clean.

On the third day the people assembled at the foot of the mountain, taking care not to get too close to it (if the identification is correct the mountain rises abruptly from a flat plain), and witnessed a scene which they interpreted as God talking with Moses:

> On the morning of the third day there were thunders and lightnings, and a thick cloud upon the mountain, and a very loud trumpet blast, so that all the people that were in the camp trembled. Then Moses brought the people out of the camp to meet God; and they took their stand at the foot of the mountain. And Mount Sinai was wrapped in smoke, because the Lord descended upon it in fire; and the smoke of it went up like the smoke of a kiln, and the whole mountain quaked greatly. And as the sound of the trumpet grew louder and louder, Moses spoke, and God answered him in thunder. And the Lord came down upon Mount Sinai, to the top of the mountain; and the Lord called Moses to the top of the mountain, and Moses went up. [Ex 19:16–20]

We are right at the heart of the Hebrew faith here, and we should tread with caution. It is no use expecting to tie it all up neatly, to define it in a well-chosen phrase and pin it out so that we know exactly what we have got. We are dealing with mystery, not problem, and although we must do all we can to understand and clarify, we cannot expect an answer to all the questions we should like to ask. We can make comparisons and draw parallels, but in the end it is like talking about someone we love: even as we penetrate further and further into their lives we know that there is infinitely more there than we can ever discover, let alone talk about. So here. We use a word to express the relationship God has established with men: 'covenant' (and this is by no means confined to Jews; the heart of the Christian belief about God and man is expressed in terms of a 'new covenant'). We must look at what this means, but as we do so let us bear constantly in mind that the words and ideas we use are no more than signposts pointing into the centre of the mystery. At that centre there are not words but silence.

The Hebrew word has a wide range of secular uses quite apart from the religious ones, to express a relationship between people. It is a common word for an alliance between nations, such as the covenant between Solomon and King Hiram of Tyre, and for an alliance between ordinary men— sometimes with no intention of keeping it, as in Hos 10:4:

> They utter mere words;
>   with empty oaths they make covenants.

It is used to express the close friendship between David and Jonathan:

> Then Jonathan made a covenant with David, because he loved him as his own soul. [1 Sm 18:3]

and the marriage bond. But it is also used to express the relationship between a king and his subjects, as when David became king of the northern group of Israelites who had been subjects of King Saul:

> Then all the tribes of Israel came to David at Hebron, and said ... The Lord said to you, You shall be shepherd of my people Israel, and you shall be prince over Israel. So all the elders of Israel came to the king at Hebron; and King David made a covenant with them at Hebron before the Lord, and they annointed David king over Israel. [2 Sm 5:1–3]

This is getting close to the usage we are looking for: a form which establishes the relationship between king and subjects and shows how each stands towards the other. A recent article by Mendenhall in the *Biblical Archaeologist* (No 17 (1954), 50–76) has drawn attention to other treaties between a sovereign and his subjects in this area of the Middle East at much the same time as the exodus. The sovereign tells of the great acts which he has done for his people, forbids any relationship between his subjects and other powers, and backs it all with blessings for being faithful to the covenant and curses for breaking it.

By combining, and extending, these uses we can begin to see what the covenant meant when it was used to express the relationship between God and his people. Firstly, the very use of such a phrase as 'his people' is significant, the covenant made the people: the nation was formed by the covenant. This is not a case of a nation accepting Yahweh as their national God: before God chose them for his people there was no nation at all, they were just a collection of tribes and clans vaguely tracing a common descent; and even this, the common descent, was very likely a belief that was at least strengthened, if not actually formed, by the covenant experience. Later, the Jews gave the appearance of believing they were Jews because of physical descent alone, and this was one of the strongest things that St Paul had to fight, as is shown by the number of times he argues about the inheritance of the promises in his letters. Letters as far apart as Galatians, 2 Corinthians, Romans, and Philippians all have passages aimed at undermining the belief that being descended from Abraham was what mattered. A passage in Romans is typical:

> For not all who are descended from Israel belong to Israel, and not all are children of Abraham because they are his descendants; but 'Through Isaac shall your descendants be named'. This means that it is not the children of the flesh who are the children of God, but the children of the promise are reckoned as descendants . . . [Rm 9:6–8, and so on for three chapters]

In this St Paul was only returning to early Hebrew practice. The nation accepted anyone who accepted the covenant, as the legislation (some of it quite late) about admitting foreigners to membership of the 'full assembly' shows. What constitutes a nation is usually a very mysterious thing, as many modern nationalist movements show, but in the case of the Jews there is no problem. The nation was made by God when he chose them and proved that he had chosen them by bringing them out of Egypt. You were a member of the nation if you had been picked out from the other people or joined yourself to those who had been picked out. There is a famous passage in the Book of Leviticus where this is expressed:

> And I will have regard for you and make you fruitful and multiply you, and will confirm my covenant with you. And you shall eat old store long kept, and you shall clear out the old to make way for the new. And I will make my abode among you, and my soul shall not abhor you. And I will walk among you, and will be your God, and you shall be my people. I am the Lord your God who brought you forth out of the land of Egypt, that you should not be their slaves; and I have broken the bars of your yoke and made you walk erect. [Lv 26:9–13]

I will be your God, and you shall be my people. It is the same kind of activity as the creation of the world, a result of God's creative power.

The second consequence of the covenant is that it created security for the people, for it contained a promise by God. There is no question of living with a God whose inexplicable anger might burst amongst his worshippers at any moment. This had a profound effect on the whole approach to worship, and is the reason why any idea of 'propitiating' God is out of the question. The basis of sacrifice for the Hebrews was communion with God, and using the divine power to maintain that communion or to restore it if it were accidentally broken. There was no question of restoring the relationship with God if it were deliberately broken by a man, that could only lead to death—'so you shall purge the evil from your midst', as the Book of Deuteronomy puts it—but this was entirely consistent and understandable; you were not having to cope with living with an unpredictable tyrant of a God. Inevitably, this security was interpreted in too materialistic a sense: 'You shall eat old store long kept, and you shall clear out the old to make way for the new', the perpetual hope of an agricultural people as expressed in the passage from Leviticus just quoted, but it also made possible the long, progressive exploration of the character of God which the prophets made, each starting from the discoveries of his predecessors.

The tradition of the covenants made with the tribal ancestors before the entry into Egypt is an expression of this security and the dependable continuity of the promises and of God's attitude to his people. 'The house of Jacob, and people of Israel' worshipped God as him who had made the promises to Abraham, Isaac, and Jacob:

> I will make of you a great nation, and I will bless you, and make your name great, so that you will be a blessing. I will bless those who bless you, and him who curses you I will curse; and in you all the nations of the earth shall be blessed. [Gn 12:2–3. See also 26:4 and 28:14]

So Moses was commanded to tell the people, 'The Lord, the God of your fathers, the God of Abraham, the God of Isaac, and the God of Jacob, has sent me to you', and, most important, he is a God of utterly consistent, unchanging character: 'This is my name for ever, and thus I am to be remembered throughout all generations' (Ex 3:15). Possession of the land became a symbol of this dependability of the promises, a guarantee that God's choice of them continued, and even during the exile when prophets of the stature of Jeremiah and Ezekiel were telling the Jews in Babylon to settle down and stop expecting a quick return to Jerusalem, there was never any doubt that there would be a return. Jeremiah, in fact, publicly bought land occupied by the Babylonians, and Ezekiel has such passages as the great picture of God as the shepherd of his people:

> I will bring them out from the peoples, and gather them from the countries, and will bring them into their own land; and I will feed them on the mountains of Israel, by the fountains, and in all the inhabited places of the country. [Ezek 34:13]

Thirdly, the covenant had an historical fact as its basis. It was not grounded in a system of thought, a theory about the nature of man and the world he inhabits, a philosophical school such as those associated with Socrates or with Epicurus, but on the evidence of God's power witnessed by those who had been slaves in Egypt and found themselves free as a result of that power. This power was ultimately seen to be the same power as had made the world and set man in it and which controlled events, and this had important consequences for the claims which God makes on man. The covenant was with the whole man, not just part of him. It was with man seen as a whole: body and soul; family, land, and all he possessed were involved in the covenant with God. There was no real distinction between sacred and secular within the covenant, no area which was 'private' to man, no aspect of human life which was beneath God's interest. This is in the sharpest possible contrast with the typical Greek view—the one which we who live in modern western society find ourselves accepting as the 'natural' way of thinking. This Greek view thinks of man as a soul forced to inhabit a limiting material body which imprisons and restricts it and hinders it from achieving its full capabilities. It speaks of the body as the tomb within which the soul is buried, and the object of life is to escape from the tomb into the freedom of immortality. 'The immortality of the soul' is a thoroughly inadequate idea if it means that only part of the man is fit for eternal life, and Hebrew thought has none of it. If there is to be full personal existence after death, the resurrection is the Hebrew way of thinking about it, though for much of their history the Hebrews did not take much interest in survival after death, for they considered that a man could achieve full satisfaction in this life and 'his name would be remembered' in his sons.

The exodus was a demonstration of power, and

the response to it was complete surrender on the part of man. From this point of view history becomes a dialogue between an all-powerful, ever-present, all-knowing God and the men who come into contact with that power. Its effects are to be seen in every event. At a crude level, those who co-operate with that power and obey it, prosper; those who resist it are overtaken by disaster. Many of the psalms express this theme:

> The dull man cannot know,
>> the stupid cannot understand this:
> that, though the wicked sprout like grass
>> and all evildoers flourish,
> they are doomed to destruction for ever,
>> but thou, O Lord, art on high for ever.
> For, lo, thy enemies, O Lord,
>> for, lo, thy enemies shall perish;
>> all evildoers shall be scattered.

> The righteous flourish like the palm tree,
>> and grow like a cedar in Lebanon.
> They are planted in the house of the Lord,
>> they flourish in the courts of our God.
> They still bring forth fruit in old age,
>> they are ever full of sap and green,
> To show that the Lord is upright;
>> he is my rock, and there is no unrighteousness
>> in him. [Ps 92:6–15]

Later it came to be seen that it is not as simple as this, that the good man often suffers, and that God works out his purposes with men who do not acknowledge him. But the principle remains secure: God is in control and is consistent, and consequently he requires from his people behaviour which reflects the character of the God who made the covenant with them.

This is the fourth consequence of the covenant. It produces law. For the language of the covenant, at any rate, no matter how patient and long-suffering God may show himself to be in practice, is conditional on the people's obedience. If they obey, God will bless:

> And because you hearken to these ordinances, and keep and do them, the Lord your God will keep with you the covenant and the steadfast love which he swore to your fathers to keep; he will love you, bless you, and multiply you; he will also bless the fruit of your body and the fruit of your ground . . . [Dt 7:12–13ff.]

In practice this means that there must be law, and that the law is part of religion. We have seen that the administration of the law was seen as an essentially priestly function when Jethro the priest gave Moses advice about judging the people's cases, when 'the people come to me to inquire of God . . . and I make them know the statutes of God and his decisions' (Ex 18:15–16). The description of the events at Mount Sinai, when the people were witnesses of the effects of the presence of God and of his conversation with their representative, Moses, is followed immediately by the Decalogue, the Ten Commandments,

with no connecting passage at all. There is no
need for any explanation of why the most important part of the law is the immediate consequence
of the covenant. It is the condition under which
the people can be partners in the relationship with
God. It is an important condition, for it gives the
people responsibility. They are not just possessions of God like so much cattle or so many
slaves. Indeed, they have been released from
slavery in order to become partners in the
covenant, and their responsibility in law is the
measure of their dignity and newly given freedom.
Their behaviour matters to God because they are
themselves of infinite value in his eyes. They are
his representatives on earth, and their lives must
be worthy of the God whom they represent.

With this in mind, the meaning of the covenant,
it is worth looking again at the four verses in
chapter 19 of Exodus where the meaning of the
covenant is stated. Perhaps we may see this as the
restatement of a theme after a composer has developed it. It is the same theme but we see more
easily what is contained in it:

> Thus you shall say to the house of Jacob, and
> tell the people of Israel: You have seen what I
> did to the Egyptians, and how I bore you on
> eagles' wings and brought you to myself. Now
> therefore, if you will obey my voice and keep
> my covenant, you shall be my own possession
> among all peoples; for all the earth is mine, and
> you shall be to me a kingdom of priests and a
> holy nation. [Ex 19:3–6]

A kingdom of priests and a holy nation. In the first account of creation at the beginning of Genesis, the creation of man is described in these words:

> Then God said, Let us make man in our image, after our likeness; and let them have dominion over the fish of the sea, and over the birds of the air, and over the cattle, and over all the earth, and over every creeping thing that creeps upon the earth. [Gn 1:26]

The image which is at work here is of an emperor appointing a governor, an administrator, in a province of his empire, and erecting a statue of himself so that the inhabitants will know whose will it is that rules them. It is picture language, and although it tells us nothing about the historical origins of man and of his place in the development of animal life, it does convey a truth of another kind. Whatever our beliefs, we behave on the assumption that man is the most important thing on this planet with the right to explore, and experiment with, and use everything around him. According to the old Hebrew traditions God intended that man should do this as his representative, so that the world could find its purpose and its peace in God through man. The intention failed because the governor rebelled. The covenant was the beginning of God's move to repair the damage and bring his world back into his peace. It is a plan with several phases to it, and the first phase was to create an area of obedience and mutual trust in the broken world of disorder and enmity, a bridgehead from which God could reach out, a centre of harmony to which the world would be drawn. This is why the newly created nation is called 'a kingdom of priests and a holy nation'. They are to mediate God to the world, and be the place where the world makes its response in the worship of God. This is what the covenant was for:

> Thus says God, the Lord,
>> who created the heavens and stretched them out,
>> who spread forth the earth and what comes from it,
> who gives breath to the people upon it
>> and spirit to those who walk in it:
> I am the Lord, I have called you in righteousness,
>> I have taken you by the hand and kept you;
> I have given you as a covenant to the people,
>> a light to the nations,
>> to open the eyes that are blind,
> to bring out the prisoners from the dungeon,
>> from the prison those who sit in darkness.
>> [Is 42:5–7]

Additional Notes

The Old Testament

The 'J' source, from the arrival on the other side of the 'Red Sea' to the covenant at Mount Sinai, is to be found in the following passages:

Ex 15:22–25, 27; 16:4–5, 13b–15, 27–30; 17:1b–3, 7ac; 18:1–5, 6b, 8b, 9b–10, 14b–16a, 19–20, 23b–25a; 19:9a, 11b–13a, 15, 18, 20–22, 24b–25.

The main references to the Sinai covenant in other books of the Old Testament are:

Lv 2:13; 24:8; 26:9, 15, 24, 44f.
Dt 4:13; 28:69; 29:20
Is 56:4, 6
Jer 11:2, 3, 6, 8, 10; 14:21; 22:9; 31:32
Ezek 16:8, 59, 60; 44:7
Dn 9:4; 11:28, 30, 32
Hos 6:7; 8:1
Zech 9:11; 11:10
(The psalm references are given at the end of chapter 7.)

But there are very many allusions to the covenant, apart from these references. Jeremiah refers to a 'new covenant', which lies in the future, in 31:31.

The New Testament

The main New Testament references are:
Mt 26:28
Mk 14:24
Lk 22:20
1 Cor 11:25
2 Cor 3:6
Heb 13:20
(The phrase 'New Testament' is the same as 'New Covenant'.)

You might like to consider: in what ways the new covenant creates our communities at the present day, gives the assurance that God's love is important and relevant, and is the foundation of human responsibility.

6

The people

What were these people like who entered the 'promised land', Canaan, the area in Palestine around the Dead Sea and the Sea of Galilee, as we now know it? We have seen that their religious obligations were expressed in law, and that the law was directly related to the character of the God whom they worshipped—or at least was an expression of what they thought their God required of them, an expression of their obligations towards him. For they were only a nation because God had made them one, and their relationships with each other, what we would now call 'human rights', were a direct product of that more funda mental relationship: the covenant between the nation and God.

People carry knowledge with them, the accumulation of knowledge acquired by hard experience: how to control and breed animals; how to solve the disputes and problems that arise within a community; how to live with neighbouring peoples; religious experience, and the memories of past history and of ancestors, which help to maintain their consciousness of themselves as a people. Where the community is closely knit and comparatively uniform in possessions and responsibilities—as, for example, a nomad tribe might be —it is possible to speak of a 'common culture'. All members of the community share in it, and all members contribute to it. The Hebrews who entered Canaan after the escape from Egypt and the journey through the desert were possessors of a common culture.

If some modern writers about our society are correct, our own culture is no longer a uniform one; it is at least divided into a scientific and a non-scientific way of thinking. If we now, in this study of the exodus, go on to separate out different aspects of the ancient Hebrew culture this must not lead us to assume that it was a divided one. The divisions exist only in our method of studying them. There was no division between Hebrew historians and Hebrew priests and Hebrew lawyers: they were usually the same men, they shared exactly the same presuppositions, and in any case the history, the religious practice, and the law were all the possession of the people as a whole, not of groups separated from them. If we forget this we shall be in danger of running into serious error. History, religion, and law all inter-penetrate and illuminate each other.

The common culture of the Hebrew people may be viewed from three aspects. They carried with them knowledge of their history. At the centre of this, now, was the knowledge of the recent events during their escape from Egypt, but there was also a whole complex of memories about the period before their ancestors filtered into Egypt, and traditions about their neighbours: how they came to be at enmity with some and friendly with others. From the religious point of view they worshipped God through sacrifices in which the use of blood, as the part of the animal which contained its life, played an important part, and particularly they had a spring festival when a lamb was sacrificed by each family. They possibly held that there were certain places which were particularly holy, or 'set apart' by God, where past members of their tribes had been particularly conscious of God's presence and had set up an altar of rough stones or a pillar. They had a simple but vividly moving account of the origins of pain, sexual shame, the enmity of wild animals, and the difficulties of raising food, in terms of man's origins in a garden where he was in harmony with God and the centre of a complete harmony of nature; but he had stolen powers which did not belong to him and God had banished him from his primitive peace. And they carried with them laws covering, as we might expect, both civil and criminal offences.

This complex tradition went through a number of processes which affected both its form and its contents. There were four points in Hebrew history where the tradition, the common culture, went into the melting pot or at least went through a process of editing and rearrangement. One was the exodus itself; another was the unification of the kingdom under David. A third occurred when the northern kingdom, Israel, was annihilated by the Assyrians, leaving only Judah, the southern kingdom. Shortly afterwards the child sacrifices and sacral prostitution of the reign of

Manasseh provoked a re-examination of this tradition, particularly the legal parts of it, which resulted in the abortive reform under King Josiah, associated with the Book of Deuteronomy; and finally the exile in Babylon, the most shattering experience in the entire history of the Jews until the destruction of Jerusalem by the Romans, stimulated a final rearrangement of it all and the addition of a framework. This framework, the work of priests in exile, was the fruit of a long, profound look at the whole history of the nation from before the exodus (by then it was as far back as the Norman Conquest is for us), and it set a profoundly theological view on the whole tradition. The result is, at least, the first seven books of the Old Testament (Genesis to Judges) more or less as we now know them.

The tradition is a complex thing, and the law is part of that complex, not a separate thing. Despite this, however, it is possible to dig out seven distinct collections of law with some confidence; they are these:

1. 'The Book of the Covenant.' Ex 20:22 – 23:19.
2. 'The Ten Commandments', sometimes called 'The Decalogue'. These are given in two slightly different forms in Ex 20:1–17 and Dt 5:6–21.
3. 'The Twelve Curses', in Dt 27:14–26.
4. 'The Ritual Decalogue', which is a collection of ten laws about feasts and sacrifices which occurs in slightly different forms in Ex 22:28–29, 23:12 and 15–29, in Ex 34:10–26, and scattered about all over Deuteronomy.

5. The Deuteronomic Code, which is the whole central section of the Book of Deuteronomy: chapters 12–26.
6. The Priestly Code, which consists of most of Leviticus and parts of Exodus and Numbers. Ezek 40–48 is closely associated with the Priestly Code.
7. The Holiness Code, which is Lv 17 – 26.

Having recognised them, how are we to decide where each one fits into the nation's history? Every one of them had been copied and recopied for hundreds of years before they reached manuscripts we now possess, and at each major period of editorial activity there is a chance that they have been changed. How *can* we decide which ones are old and which are late?

Fortunately, there are a number of clues we can use. During the last century a great deal of legal material has been dug up (literally) all over the Middle East, and some of it has survived from a very early date—two thousand or more years BC in some cases—because it was written on clay, which was then baked, or carved in stone. The Hebrews used pen and ink on less durable materials: leather or papyrus paper. In this very ancient legal material there is a recognisable grammatical form used, and a consistent pattern, in some cases, and where this form or pattern occurs in Hebrew laws it is probable that we have very old laws. Fortunately, the Hebrew scribes who did the copying were extraordinarily careful to copy exactly what they had in front of them (and there was an extremely complex system of checks, such as counting letters, to make sure they had made no mistake), so the different grammatical forms have survived. An example may help to make all this clearer. The oldest laws used a 'third person singular' form, such as 'he that hits a man'; more recent ones move to the 'second person singular', such as 'if thou lend money' (the modern English use of 'you' for both the singular and plural forms of the verb obscures this distinction), and more recent laws still use the 'second person plural', such as 'you shall be holy men unto me'. So, two successive verses in Ex 22 show laws belonging to three different periods, if notice is taken of the form of the Hebrew:

He that sacrifices to any God, except only to the Lord, shall be given over to destruction. And thou shalt not wrong a stranger, nor oppress him: for you were strangers in the land of Egypt. [Ex 22:20–21]

There are other clues too, and even late collections of laws sometimes quote much earlier laws. The Book of Deuteronomy, for example, which was not compiled until at least six hundred years after the exodus, sometimes gives ancient laws because they have been left out of the collections of laws already existing.

This still does not enable us to date the earliest parts at all precisely, of course, and there is a particularly vexing problem about the law of the non-Hebrew people already living in Canaan when the Hebrews arrived there after the exodus. The

Hebrews took over a number of their laws, it seems; how are we to know which they were? Does it matter? It does indeed, for if we are looking for the influence of the covenant and the exodus experience on the people's law, we should like to know what the law was before they settled in Canaan. There are some clues here, however. The Canaanites were an agricultural people who raised crops on settled ground, while the Hebrews were a shepherd people moving their flocks and herds from place to place. So wherever there is reference to crops, or to agricultural animals such as oxen, or to harvest feasts, even when it is in the ancient form it is likely to show Canaanite influence. Or, to put it more accurately, it shows that the Hebrews absorbed Canaanite living techniques into their own lives. The danger was that they would also absorb the Canaanite attitude to religion, particularly the fertility cults, and this was the long battle the prophets fought.

With these assumptions in mind, then, we find the Hebrews of the early years of the covenant had a body of law which stressed the importance and dignity and rights of the individual person. With the exception of the distinction between free men and slaves, all men were equal before the law—in sharp contrast to the laws we know of from surrounding peoples, and even the slavery was of a mild form, for it arose from debt or the failure to restore stolen property, and the slave had to be released after seven years. There is a close parallel here with the story of Jacob, for he gave Laban seven years' labour in order to marry his daughter

Rachel. Nor could the Hebrew get round the law by selling his slave to a foreigner. We might contrast this with the Roman system, at least until the first century AD, where a master could do what he wanted with his slaves, including deliver them to the beasts in the arena, and where a slave had to be given torture if he was called as a witness in the courts, to make sure he was telling the truth.

Other codes of the period contain extensive mutilation as punishments but the Hebrew codes are impressively free from this. Apart from the death penalty other crimes or accidents are met by a system of restoration or compensation. The only major exception to this, the *lex talionis* of 'an eye for an eye and a tooth for a tooth', is in fact a law *limiting* the amount of vengeance a man can get away with, as its name shows. 'Talionis' is from the Latin 'talis', meaning 'the like', and the law means that if a man does more injury to another than the other has done to him he will be punished for it.

A wide range of injury and loss to others is covered, and after damage to the person has been covered, the law deals with damage to property and theft. There is also a section forbidding sacrifice to any God but Yahweh. All this is to be found in the ancient parts of 'The Book of the Covenant', the section of law closely associated with the description of the events at Mount Sinai in Exodus 20 – 23, and it is worth noticing that the order of the laws reverses the order of such codes as that of Hammurabi, the early Babylonian king of about 1700 BC, for it puts the law of the person first, apart from being a good deal more humane.

Also very old are the laws cast in a very brief, repetitive form where each phrase contains the same number of words or is so worded that it can easily be remembered. The 'Twelve Curses' in Dt 27 belong to this kind of law and in this case are a solution to the problem of undetected crime; the community discharges its responsibility before God by solemnly cursing the undiscovered criminal and disassociating itself from his crime. The law of capital offences is cast in a similar form, and we may assume that they belong to a period before writing had come into extensive use. We can also see this as the underlying form in the Ten Commandments. These have clearly been expanded and worked over by successive editors, particularly the editors of the Deuteronomic period, but we can be confident that the main pattern of them and the teaching they contain is very old, and from what we know of the Canaanite religion, we can be confident that it is not the source of this law.

Although we cannot have the degree of certainty about all this that we would like, there is sufficient to be able to notice a profound difference between these early Hebrews and their contemporaries in other societies. Their law was a reflection of the God whom they worshipped. As he was righteous, predictable, equitable, so his people acknowledged that in their relationships with each other they too must be accountable for their actions—no matter who they were or how important a position they occupied—by a code of behaviour which all understood and accepted, which held men to their promises and respected the person and property of the other members of the society. Years later a Hebrew king wanted the wife of one of his subjects. Anywhere in the Middle East the problem was one with a simple solution, and David followed the common pattern. He arranged for the man to be killed and he took his wife. A man with God's viewpoint took it upon himself to face David with his crime. He put a case to him:

> ... Now there came a traveller to the rich man, and he was unwilling to take one of his own flock or herd to prepare for the wayfarer who had come to him, but he took the poor man's lamb, and prepared it for the man who had come to him. Then David's anger was greatly kindled against the man (in the story); and he said to Nathan, As the Lord lives, the man who has done this deserves to die; and he shall restore the lamb fourfold, because he did the thing, and because he had no pity.
>
> Nathan said to David, You are the man. Thus says the Lord, the God of Israel, I anointed you king over Israel ... Why have you despised the word of the Lord, to do what is evil in his sight? [2 Sm 12:4–9. In some Catholic translations this will be 2 Kgs]

Law in its abstract form is a tedious thing, except for lawyers, but one case can bring it to life, and so does this one. It is the spirit of Moses and the law he mediated to the people. There is an absolute standard of righteousness at work here, a standard which applies to all men; David did not need to ask who the man was before he came to a conclusion about him, he did not have to find out if he was a high officer of state, or a member of the nobility, or a large landowner—as an Assyrian or Babylonian or Egyptian king would have had to—before he could deliver judgement. All men are equal before David's God, including David himself. Then the law is obvious and predictable, a matter of ordinary rational judgement, if those under the law are subjects of the God who is the living one and who shares his life with them. For this is the heart of the matter: the crime is against God, for everything in the nation comes from God and is answerable to him; David's kingship, the rich man's wealth and the poor man's lamb, all come from God, and the use made of them is God's business:

> David said to Nathan, I have sinned against the Lord. And Nathan said to David, The Lord has also put away your sin; you shall not die. Nevertheless, because by this deed you have utterly scorned the Lord . . . [2 Sm 12:13–14]

Crime was not just an offence against society, it was a sin against the God who had rescued them and made them into a people. It was the only true motive for keeping the law. The Hebrews obtained their laws from a wide variety of sources and peoples, as well as from their own experience. It is not the origin of the law that matters; it is what the Hebrews did with it when they had got it. They added motive to it; the reason for keeping the law was rooted in the covenant experience. One example is enough. It is no use releasing a slave if this only means adding one more poverty-stricken landless man to the community; that can only lead to theft and robbery. It is only common sense that a released slave must be given the means of living: a job, or property, or at least something to keep him going until he can find his feet. So Hebrew law made provision for this. But notice carefully the *reason* it gives:

> If your brother, a Hebrew man, or a Hebrew woman, is sold to you, he shall serve you six years, and in the seventh year you shall let him go free from you. And when you let him go free from you, you shall not let him go empty-handed; you shall furnish him liberally out of your flock, out of your threshing floor, and out of your wine press; as the Lord your God has blessed you, you shall give to him. You shall remember that you were a slave in the land of Egypt, and the Lord your God redeemed you; therefore I command you this today. [Dt 15:12–15]

The Lord your God redeemed you. This view of the situation was communicated to the people by Moses. It is time we looked at the place the man Moses occupies in the tradition of the exodus.

The exodus itself is the measure of his stature. At the level of leadership alone he successfully brought his people out of Egypt and gave them the impetus which carried them into Canaan and enabled them to settle there. He was helped in this by the distant background of nomadic desert life in the memory of the people; when he led them out into the desert he was not asking them to do something never heard of in their history. Just as the English think of themselves as seafarers, so the Hebrews thought of themselves as desert dwellers, yet the harsh reality of it, an entirely new experience in the lives of most of those who took part, quickly brought a rebellious attitude to the surface, and this becomes a recurring theme in the traditions:

> And the whole congregation of the people of Israel murmured against Moses and Aaron in the wilderness, and said to them, Would that we had died by the hand of the Lord in the land of Egypt, when we sat by the fleshpots and ate bread to the full; for you have brought us out into this wilderness to kill this whole assembly with hunger. [Ex 16:2-3]

And again,

> But the people thirsted there for water, and the people murmured against Moses, and said, Why did you bring us up out of Egypt, to kill us and our children and our cattle with thirst? So Moses cried to the Lord, What shall I do with this people? They are almost ready to stone me. [Ex 17:3-4]

So strong is this theme, in fact, that part of the tradition makes it the cause of the length of time the people were in the wilderness before entering

Canaan. They were to be forty years about it so
that all those who had complained should die in
the desert and only their children enter the
promised land:

> And the Lord said to Moses and Aaron, How
> long shall this wicked congregation murmur
> against me? . . . Say to them, As I live, says the
> Lord, . . . your dead bodies shall fall in this
> wilderness. And your children shall be shep-
> herds in the wilderness forty years, and shall
> suffer for your faithlessness, until the last of
> your dead bodies lies in the wilderness. [Nm 14:
> 26–33]

Under his leadership, humanly speaking, the
people left Egypt as a dispirited group of slaves,
and entered the promised land a nation with a
tradition and pride which laid the foundation for
the national consciousness which is still strong today. In this achievement Moses shows the character of a king.

He exercised many of the functions normally
associated with sovereignty, except that the place
given to God in the national life turned these functions into those of a priest. The administration of
law and the delegation of responsibility were seen
as the means by which God's will could be
mediated to the people, and so became priestly
acts. We have already seen something of this in
the discussion about Jethro, but there are other
places where Moses' activity was priestly. He
talked directly with God, and told the people what
God wanted them to do; and there are several

occasions when the tradition depicts him pleading for God to have mercy on the people when they have angered him:

> But Moses besought the Lord his God, and said, O Lord, why does thy wrath burn hot against thy people, whom thou hast brought forth out of the land of Egypt with great power and with a mighty hand?... Remember Abraham, Isaac, and Israel, thy servants, to whom thou didst swear by thine own self, and didst say to them, I will multiply your descendants as the stars of heaven, and all this land that I have promised I will give to your descendants, and they shall inherit it for ever. And the Lord repented of the evil which he thought to do to his people. [Ex 32:11–14]

The whole of the priestly tradition's instructions about sacrifice and the temple and its furnishings are written as if they had come from the mouth of Moses himself. No doubt the authors of this, writing seven hundred years after the exodus, knew well that a great deal of the detail of the temple traditions had appeared long after Moses, and they are writing in what we would now call 'the spirit of Moses'; but in doing so they clearly believed that Moses had authority in the priestly sphere. It is interesting, for example, that they put it all into Moses' mouth, and not Aaron's, for although Aaron was the ancestor of all priests, he only exercised his priesthood as Moses' representative:

> He shall speak for you to the people; and he

shall be a mouth for you, and you shall be to him as God. [Ex 4:16]

The whole attitude is rather as if we wrote all our theory of naval strategy and tactics as if it were Nelson speaking—but it would be into Nelson's mouth that we put the words, not Wellington's. The only surprising thing is that there is never an instance of Moses actually sacrificing, but this is because Aaron is his representative and also, more importantly, because at this period in the nation's history it was the head of each family who offered the sacrifices, as we have seen in the case of the Passover. Sacrificing was not yet a function which only a priest could perform, and in the case of the Passover it never did become so.

But Moses' most conspicuous achievement lay in the viewpoint he communicated to the people about God. The most important thing about a prophet is not that he can see into the future, nor that he shows he is 'possessed' by some force from outside, but that he can see his own situation from God's point of view. By this definition Moses must be seen as the first and most outstanding of the prophets, for he it was who saw the hand of God at work in the events of the exodus, who managed to get the people to see those events from that point of view, and who got the people to turn this faith into action. It was the first, and the decisive, step towards the position from which God could be seen present and active in history, and from then onwards the whole of the nation's history was seen as the interaction between God and his people. Later, under the influence first of the expansion of the Assyrian military power and later of the exile in Babylon, that interaction was seen to extend into the whole world.

In the end this was accepted as the real mark of the prophet: that he was the man who applied Moses' vision to the circumstances of his own time. Moses' vision was an understanding which extended in two directions: he became aware of the character of the God who had called him, and chosen his people, and set him over them with the task of communicating his knowledge, his vision, to them. And he understood his own times, so that he saw what the God whom he worshipped wanted of his people. It was an obedience and response which should extend into every corner of their lives and every detail of their dealings with each other. It is this which is the mark of all the great prophets of Israel, from Nathan, who rebuked David, right through to Jeremiah, Ezekiel, and the great anonymous prophet who lived at the end of the period of exile in Babylon, the man who saw further than anyone else in the Old Testament into the nature of suffering. The view which Moses communicated became the true test for the authenticity of prophecy, so that even if a prophet could work miracles and foretell the future he was to be rejected if his teaching contradicted the Mosaic tradition:

If a prophet arises among you, or a dreamer of dreams, and gives you a sign or a wonder, and the sign or wonder which he tells you comes to

pass, and if he says, Let us go after other gods
(which you have not known), and let us serve
them, you shall not listen to the words of that
prophet or that dreamer of dreams ... You
shall walk after the Lord your God and fear
him, and keep his commandments and obey his
voice, and you shall serve him and cleave to
him. But that prophet or that dreamer of dreams
shall be put to death, because he has taught rebellion against the Lord your God, who brought
you out of the land of Egypt and redeemed you
out of the house of bondage ... [Dt 13:1-5]

'The Lord your God, who brought you out of
the land of Egypt and redeemed you ...' This is
the viewpoint which Moses left as his legacy to
his people: the fact for faith on which their lives
and the lives of their successors was to be
grounded. It was the one thing which distinguished
their religion from that of their neighbours. Their
God had revealed himself decisively in their history, he had shown that he had the power, and
that his rule was to be a righteous rule over
righteous people. Often in the course of their history the people deviated from that ideal, but
always the tradition Moses had started, the viewpoint he had communicated, was there as a standard. All their subsequent experience they
attributed to Moses, for it all grew from the seed
he planted amongst them, the experience he had
of God. This is the true mark of his greatness. The
people who came from the desert into Canaan
carried that viewpoint with them.

Additional notes

The Old Testament

Examples of codes of law in the Old Testament are to be found in the following passages:

Ex 20:1–17; Dt 5:6–21 'The Ten Commandments.' The main difference between these two versions is that the Exodus one makes the seventh-day rest a commemoration of the creation, while the one in Deuteronomy gives humanitarian reasons for it, and makes it a commemoration of the exodus from Egypt.

Ex 20:22 – 23:33 'The Book of the Covenant.' This is an ancient collection of civil and criminal law, probably the oldest collection in the bible.

Dt 12 –16 'The Code of Deuteronomy.' This is a collection made secretly during the reign of Manasseh in the first half of the seventh century BC. It makes the escape from Egypt the motive for keeping the law, and was the basis of Josiah's reform in 621.

Lv 17:1 – 26:46 'The Holiness Code.' This gets its name from the stress it lays on holiness; it probably shows the influence of Ezekiel (see Ezek 36:22–38), and is this later than Deuteronomy.

The New Testament

Some of the main passages about law in the New Testament are to be found in:

Mt 5:17–20 'I have come not to abolish (the law) but to fulfil . . .'

Mt 5:21 – 8:27 'The Sermon on the Mount.'

Mk 12:28–31   Christ's summary of the whole law into two commandments: duty to God and to one's neighbour.

Rm 7 – 8:11   St Paul's discussion of 'the law of the Spirit', compared with the Jewish law, and the 'law of sin and death'.

Gal 3:15–29   The Jewish law seen as a 'guardian', which was no longer needed once Christ had come.

In the above, 'law' is best understood as 'a way of life' or 'a particular pattern of behaviour', rather than a set of rules.

A number of Christ's parables are to be found in Lk 14 – 17:10. Nathan's parable to David is in 2 Sm (2 Kgs) 12:1–15.

You might like to consider: how modern legislation about the dignity, rights, and responsibilities of the individual, and of the community, are related to the life and work of Christ.

7

The promised land

Canaan already had people living in it. What happened when the Israelites appeared from the eastern desert? We have two accounts of the events, one in the Book of Joshua, the other in the Book of Judges; in their present form they look as if one carries on with the story where the other ends. Joshua deals, it seems, with the events immediately following the entry of the people and Judges carries on after the death of Joshua. Incidentally, 'judge' is a misleading word to use, 'chief' would convey the meaning better; the men described were essentially local leaders each of whom emerged in response to a particular emergency. They did administer the law, but only because they had won their position on the battle-field. The Book of Joshua describes how the people occupied the country in a series of sweeping campaigns, almost without any setback except for temporary checks through direct disobedience of the revealed will of God. In the Book of Judges, on the other hand, the situation is very different: part of the country was never under Hebrew control, and it is very difficult to see the situation as a mere 'mopping-up' period after a successful campaign. In fact, what we seem to have in these two books is not an account of two stages in the settlement in Canaan, but rather two different versions of the *same* stage: one which makes the Hebrews irresistible and one which sees their occupation more as a penetration than a conquest.

It is possible to account for this if we notice something of the forces which influenced the authors of the Book of Joshua. They were writing at a time when the nation had been brought to the point of disaster through tolerating and encouraging foreign cults. It reached its climax in the seventh century BC when foreign alliances and corrupt Hebrew kings opened the flood-gates to a wide range of alien religions and obscene and cruel customs. The Canaanite religion itself was a fertility cult, with sacred prostitution at its centre, and with this the religion of the covenant could in the end have no compromise. Whoever wrote the Book of Joshua was anxious to emphasise that God wanted his people to have no part in this, so he depicted the conquest of the promised land as a ruthless campaign in which every trace of heathen worship, and every person who practised it, were destroyed. The attitude of these Deuteronomic historians may be seen from a passage in Deuteronomy itself, where the policy is put into the mouth of Moses:

In the cities of these peoples that the Lord your God gives you for an inheritance, you shall save alive nothing that breathes, but you shall utterly destroy them, the Hittites and the Amorites, the

Canaanites and the Perizzites, the Hivites and the Jebusites, as the Lord your God has commanded; that they may not teach you to do according to all their abominable practices which they have done in the service of their gods, and so to sin against the Lord your God. [Dt 20:16–18]

The point of this policy is contained in the last sentence. The Book of Joshua is this policy worked out in terms of the detailed campaign. At the beginning, in a passage where God speaks to Joshua, Moses' law is referred to, and without doubt it is the passage in Deuteronomy that the author had in mind:

Be strong and of good courage; for you shall cause this people to inherit the land which I swore to their fathers to give them. Only be strong and very courageous, being careful to do according to all the law which Moses my servant commanded you; turn not from it to the right hand nor to the left, that you may have good success wherever you go. [Jos 1:6–7]

The main body of the book has plenty of detail showing this policy put into effect:

And Joshua passed on from Libnah, and all Israel with him, to Lachish, and laid siege to it, and assaulted it: and the Lord gave Lachish into the hand of Israel, and he took it on the second day, and smote it with the edge of the sword, and every person in it, as he had done to Libnah. [Jos 10:31–32] and so on for city after city. It is safer to see in all this the horror of men who have seen human sacrifice become common, along with much else, rather than accept this version as an historical account of how the land was settled. It is really a comment on the early part of the seventh century, not the twelfth.

Even in the Book of Joshua there are the occasional inconsistencies which show that it was not a complete conquest: Gezer and Jerusalem remain in the hands of their own people; but it is in the Book of Judges that we begin to get a more likely picture. The second half of Jg 1 is a long list of places which the Israelites failed to capture. Compared with the contour lines on a map, they give an interesting result: they are all either ports or they lie in the fertile valleys and central lowlands, except for a belt of country running right across the centre and including the hilly area where Jerusalem is. This is supported by the text, for twice there are references to failure to capture areas down in the plains: '... but he could not drive out the inhabitants of the plain, because they had chariots of iron' (Jg 1:19), and 'The Amorites pressed the Danites back into the hill country, for they did not allow them to come down to the plain' (Jg 1:34). It is all summed up quite plainly:

> So the people of Israel dwelt among the Canaanites, the Hittites, the Amorites, the Perizzites, the Hivites, and the Jebusites; and they took their daughters to themselves for

wives, and their own daughters they gave to their sons; and they served their gods. [Jg 3:5–6]

It was not a conquest but an infiltration. The Hebrews and their flocks took over the high ground where there was grazing sufficient for their needs, and the agricultural Canaanites continued to cultivate the fertile plain areas.

It was the crucial test for the strength of the people's loyalty to God. In the end it led to a deepening of their understanding of the God who had chosen them, a deepening which finally resulted in the realisation that there is only one God and that all life is dependent on him. But the immediate consequence was that the Canaanite fertility cults gained ground amongst the Hebrews:

And the people of Israel did what was evil in the sight of the Lord and served the Baals; and they forsook the Lord, the God of their fathers, who had brought them out of the land of Egypt; they went after other gods, from among the gods of the peoples who were round about them, and bowed down to them; and they provoked the Lord to anger. They forsook the Lord, and served the Baals and the Ashtaroth. [Jg 2:11–13]

It is very doubtful whether the people did in fact desert Yahweh when they began to take part in the Baal rites. For the Baalim were the 'lords' of the crops; every field would have its minor Baal, and every village its more important Baal who controlled the fertility of the district. The Ashtaroth were the consorts of the Baalim. Yahweh, for the Israelites, was still essentially a shepherd god, and his chief sacrifice was the Passover lamb. As the people mixed and intermarried with the Canaanites they learned their agricultural techniques, and with those techniques of ploughing and sowing and harvesting they naturally accepted the gods whom the Canaanites thought governed the crops.

The influence of the Canaanite religion can be seen quite early in a set of laws sometimes called 'The Ritual Decalogue'. It exists in a number of forms, and is concerned with festivals and sacrifices. Shorn of later editorial additions, it probably contained:

1. Six days you shall do your work, but on the seventh day you shall rest.
2. You shall keep the feast of unleavened bread; as I commanded you, you shall eat unleavened bread for seven days at the appointed time in the month of Abib. None shall appear before me empty-handed.
3. You shall keep the feast of harvest, of the first fruits of your labour.
4. You shall keep the feast of ingathering at the end of the year.
5. Three times in the year shall all your males appear before the Lord. (Note: 'Lord' here is 'adhon', not Yahweh.)
6. The first-born of your sons you shall give to me. You shall do likewise with your oxen and with your sheep.
7. You shall not offer the blood of my sacrifice with leavened bread.

8. You shall not let the fat of my feast remain until the morning.
9. The first of the first fruits of your ground you shall bring into the house of your God.
10. You shall not boil a kid in its mother's milk.

(These are taken from Ex 22 and 23.)

Some of these are obviously connected with the harvest, the significance of others has been lost, but the important thing is the use the Hebrews made of these laws. In fact they assimilated them and ultimately attached them to the worship of Yahweh so that they became his feasts and part of his sacrificial cult.

More significantly, they attached them to Yahweh's worship in such a way that the whole system of harvest festivals became a commemoration of the exodus and the covenant. This is an extraordinary thing to have achieved, and is yet another piece of evidence testifying to the strength of the exodus experience. The link which made it possible was the simultaneous occurrence of three things. At the same time in the month Abib the Passover became due, the escape from Egypt took place, and the Canaanites celebrated their feast of Unleavened Bread. The link-up was helped by the coincidence that unleavened bread, the normal bread of the nomad, also figured in the Passover rite. The result was that the Hebrews attached the Canaanite feast of Unleavened Bread to the Passover; it began the day after the Passover was sacrificed. Possibly the Canaanites kept a feast of Unleavened Bread at the spring sowing period through a belief that the fermenting action of yeast represented a kind of corruption, and the fertility of the crop required that they disassociated themselves from it, but whatever the reason, the Hebrews attached to it a reason of their own: the hasty flight from Egypt when there was no time to wait for the dough to rise before baking it. The motive for keeping the feast is made clear in Exodus:

> And you shall observe the feast of unleavened bread, for on this very day I brought your hosts out of the land of Egypt: therefore you shall observe this day, throughout your generations, as an ordinance for ever. [Ex 12:17]

The other Canaanite agricultural harvest festivals were all tied to the first feast of the year, Unleavened Bread, and occurred at fixed periods of time after it. So the effect of tying Unleavened Bread to the Passover was to make the whole system of agricultural feasts into memorials of the exodus.

Just how long this took is not known for certain, but the earliest strand of the tradition already has the whole system in its complete form, so it probably happened very quickly. Of great influence was the sanctuary at Shechem which seems to have been the chief of the Hebrew sanctuaries and the focal centre of the nation's religion during the early years of the settlement. Twice in the Book of Joshua there are descriptions of a solemn renewal of the covenant either at Shechem or just to the north of it:

And the people said to Joshua, The Lord our God we will serve, and his voice we will obey. So Joshua made a covenant with the people that day, and made statutes and ordinances for them at Shechem. And Joshua wrote these words in the book of the law of God; and he took a great stone, and set it up there under the oak in the sanctuary of the Lord. And Joshua said to all the people, Behold, this stone shall be a witness against us, for it has heard all the words of the Lord which he spoke to us; therefore it shall be a witness against you, lest you deal falsely with your God. [Jos 24:24–27]

If this is so, and there is wide acceptance of this point of view, the religious bond was the only unifying factor holding together the loose federation of tribes. Moreover, the purpose of the central sanctuary was to provide a permanent site for the periodic commemoration of the exodus events. The common tradition the people had carried with them was to be transmitted to their descendants. It was to be more than a transmission of dead and static history, it was to be the core around which the whole of the nation's traditions were to form, the backbone for the organisation and growth of the nation's religious experience, her life with the God who had chosen them. It was thus the foundation for a true common culture which could grow organically from this embryo.

There is yet another extraordinary piece of evidence which points to the power of this central fact in the tradition. It seems very probable that only a part of the people who came to think of themselves as one nation had in fact been to Egypt and taken part in the exodus escape. It looks as if only some of the tribes, the 'Joseph' tribes who settled in the northern part of the country, had actually experienced the exodus and the original covenant. The southern group of tribes who settled in the northern part of the settlers in Palestine some two hundred years or so before the exodus and remained there all through. There is a wide range of evidence to suggest this, both from within the bible and from external sources. Egyptian documents of the fifteenth century BC refer to groups of people with very similar names to the Hebrews moving into the Palestine area; prisoners of war from the region seem to have been Hebrews; references in texts discovered in the northern part of Palestine suggest that Hebrews were settled there long before the probable date of the exodus in the thirteenth century BC. The evidence is far from certain, but it does begin to make a coherent picture. Within the bible it is clear that the southern part of Canaan was not occupied by the Hebrews at first, for the central sanctuary was in the north, at Shechem, and the central area of the country, which included Jerusalem, was not fully occupied until the time of David, for David captured Jerusalem from the Jebusites and made it his capital. It was a masterly *political* move, for it gave the people a neutral capital midway between the northern group of tribes and the southern, and without political or religious associations for either group. The nation had its first political, as distinct from religious, unification under David—and at the death of his son Solomon the nation split into two kingdoms, a northern and a southern. If the northern and southern peoples had arrived in the country separately it would help to explain the tensions between them and the line along which the split occurred.

The events in the Book of Judges support this view too, for the southern tribes do not figure in the main campaigns, particularly the great campaign of Deborah and Barak against Sisera. The 'song of Deborah' in Jg 5 makes no mention of the southern group in its paean of praise for the tribes; this makes sense if the central part of the country was still firmly in Canaanite hands and if the Hebrew people in the southern part had not entered the country with the northerners. Moreover, in the accounts of the settlement there is a tradition of Judah penetrating from 'the city of palms' into the southern parts of the country (Jg 1:16) and settling there. 'The city of palms' could be Jericho, but it could equally be Tamar, which literally means 'palm tree', a city in the south of Judah; if it does (and my mind inclines that way) then Judah penetrated into the country from the south. Hence the traditions, too, of an abortive attempt by the tribes to get in from the south (Nm 21:1–3), which does not make sense as it stands, and the existence of the belt of Canaanite territory across the middle of the country.

That reference to the people of Judah moving into the south of the country from the city of palms is an interesting one:

> And the descendants of the Kenites, Moses'
> father-in-law, went up with the people of Judah
> from the city of palms into the wilderness of
> Judah, which lies in the Negeb near Arad; and
> they went and settled with the people. [Jg 1:16]

It is interesting because it gives us the religious
link between the Judah people in the south and
the 'Joseph' people in the north who had been in
Egypt. If they were closely associated with
Kenites, then it is very probable indeed that they
were worshippers of Yahweh. Their religious
situation would be that of Jethro before he heard
of the exodus, and like him they would accept the
news of the exodus as evidence that their god was
stronger than they had realised. 'Now I know that
Yahweh is greater than all gods', Jethro had cried
when Moses told him about the exodus, and this
would be the reaction of the southern Hebrews
when their cousins, filtering into the northern
parts of Canaan, made contact with them and
told them what had happened. They would have
no difficulty about accepting the covenant as their
own too, for it was their God who had made it
with people related to them, and, again, it speaks
for the strength of the exodus and covenant tradition. When David, who was of the tribe of Judah,
fled from the enmity of Saul, he finally made
Hebron, the great southern sanctuary, the centre
from which he worked. Perhaps here we can see
the religious centre for the southern group of
tribes corresponding with Shechem for the northern group. The whole idea is certainly one which

goes a very long way towards making the complex traditions understandable.

When did all this happen? The Hebrews were employed on store cities in the delta area of Egypt; Moses fled under one Pharaoh and returned when he died to lead the people out. Rameses II of Egypt reigned for sixty-six years from 1290 to 1224 BC, and he was followed by Merneptah. The most likely date for the exodus seems to be shortly after the end of the reign of Rameses II, for he built extensively in the delta area and the Egyptian records suggest that his successor may have been a weaker ruler. If the suggestions that it was Rameses II who chose the site of Zoan (sometimes called Tanis or Avaris) then this is conclusive, for it is one of the places where the Hebrews were put to work. But the evidence is so slight, particularly the essential archaeological evidence, that one cannot be certain.

The whole of the rest of the Old Testament is dominated by the exodus experience. That is a sweeping statement, for it covers the writings of very nearly a thousand years. Nevertheless it is true. It would be possible to cite passage after passage from writers spanning the whole range of Old Testament life and history to illustrate it. But there is a more convincing place where this may be seen: not in authors who have left their names on their work, or who can be set in a particular historical context, but in the place where the religious belief of the ordinary anonymous Israelite has come down to us: the psalms. No one can say for certain when the psalms were written; some may go back to David, others may not have been written until well after the exile in Babylon. Indeed, it is probably a mistaken approach to ask when they were written; like hymns which speak to people's hearts, they emerged and were found to express what people wanted to express in their prayer, and so they survived. Every one of them has stood the test of, by now, thousands of years of use in public worship and private devotion, and they have proved themselves effective. The exodus experience and the covenant which came out of it are central to the psalms:

> In the sight of their fathers he wrought marvels
>   in the land of Egypt, in the fields of Zoan.
> He divided the sea and let them pass through it,
>   and made the waters stand like a heap.
> In the daytime he led them with a cloud,
>   and all the night with a fiery light.
> He cleft rocks in the wilderness,
>   and gave them drink abundantly as from the
>   deep.
> He made streams come out of the rock,
>   and caused waters to flow down like rivers.
> [Ps 78:12–16]

In another, the image of growth is used—and how apt it is! The exodus was only the beginning of it all, the point from which the nation's life began and flourished:

Thou didst bring a vine out of Egypt;
　　thou didst drive out the nations and plant it.
Thou didst clear the ground for it;
　　it took deep root and filled the land.
The mountains were covered with its shade,
　　the mighty cedars with its branches;
It sent out its branches to the sea,
　　and its shoots to the river.
[Ps 80:8–11]

It was the proof of God's utterly dependable love for them, the fulfilment of the promises and the sure sign that he would always remain faithful. They gave it the same importance as the very creation of the world, and one of the psalms mentions it in the same breath. It is a psalm where the old original form has survived intact, for it was normal for the people to have a response or refrain which they could sing or say between the sections sung by the cantors at the temple services, or the synagogues, or the local sanctuaries where the psalms emerged:

O give thanks to the Lord of lords,
　　　　for his steadfast love endures for ever;
to him who alone does great wonders,
　　　　for his steadfast love endures for ever;
... to him who made the great lights,
　　　　for his steadfast love endures for ever;
the sun to rule over the day,
　　　　for his steadfast love endures for ever;
the moon and stars to govern the night,
　　　　for his steadfast love endures for ever;

to him who smote the first-born of Egypt,
>   for his steadfast love endures for ever;
and brought Israel out from among them,
>   for his steadfast love endures for ever;
[Ps 136:3–11]

and so on.

The sense of the continual care and presence of God is the legacy Israel brought away from the exodus; his choice of them, they felt, continued. It is worth noticing the present tense used about it:

>Praise the lord, O Jerusalem!
>   Praise your God, O Zion!
>For he strengthens the bars of your gates;
>   he blesses your sons within you.
>He makes peace in your borders;
>   he fills you with the finest of the wheat.
>He sends forth his command to the earth;
>   his word runs swiftly . . .
>He declares his word to Jacob,
>   his statutes and ordinances to Israel.
>He has not dealt thus with any nation;
>   they do not know his ordinances.
>Praise the Lord! [Ps 147:12–20]

It was indeed the fact for the people's faith, the rock on which they built, the unmoving certainty to which they returned in their troubles.

Additional notes

Explicit references to the events of the exodus and the covenant are to be found in the following places in the Psalms:

18:16–19; 25:14; 33:12; 37:11, 22, 29, 34; 44:1–3, 17; 50:5, 16; 66:6, 12; 68:7–18; 74:2, 13, 20; 77:15–20; 78:12–55; 80:8–11; 81:5–10; 95:8–11; 99:6–9; 103:7; 105:8–45; 106:7–45; 111:5, 9; 114:1–8; 135:8–12; 136:10–22. (The Revised Standard Version numbering is used throughout.)

Apart from these direct references there are allusions to the exodus whenever such phrases as 'wondrous things', 'steadfast love', 'mighty works', and 'victory over kings' occur, which is very frequently.

You might like to consider: how far such experiences as the concentration camps, race riots, Hiroshima, and Viet Nam help us to understand the crucifixion; also where the distinction between sacred and secular can still be made.

8

Epilogue

The principle of the exodus and the covenant is life out of death. The God who, above all, lives and acts with power, acted to create a nation out of the hopelessness of a group of insignificant Egyptian slaves. It is the same creative activity as the original and continuous creative power of God which brings being out of nothingness, order out of chaos, and which maintains his creation in being. Always the pattern is the same. It is God who must act, for man has no power of his own. When he turns away from God all power for good and harmony and peace seeps away.

When the greatest of the Hebrew writers looked into the future, they realised that the work of restoration begun in Abraham and the escape from Egypt and the covenant in the desert would have to be completed by an act of God's power which would restore man's very nature. The exodus had demonstrated his power, the covenant had given his people principles of action and law, but it was still beyond man's power to return the steadfast love which God poured into his world. For that there would have to be a new covenant.

Regularly, the nation renewed the covenant. They probably did it annually at a ceremony when the whole account of the exodus was recounted to the people. Certainly they did it at times of crisis as a symbol of the nation's desire to renew its loyalty to God. After one such moment, when Josiah tried to reform the nation in a great purging campaign which swept through the whole country—and which failed—Jeremiah wrote:

> Can the Ethiopian change his skin
> or the leopard his spots?
> Then also you can do good
> who are accustomed to evil . . .
> Woe to you, O Jerusalem!
> How long will it be
> before you are made clean? [Jer 13:23-27]

It was beyond man's power to keep God's law. So Jeremiah looked forward to a new covenant, for he knew that God would not leave his people helpless; he would bring them to the peace and rest they longed for:

> Thus says the Lord:
> The people who survived the sword
> found grace in the wilderness;
> When Israel sought for rest,
> the Lord appeared to him from afar.
> I have loved you with an everlasting love;
> therefore I have continued my faithfulness to
>   you.
> Again I will build you, and you shall be built,
> O virgin Israel. [Jer 31:2-4]

The restoration of her virginity could indeed only be achieved by God, but he would remake their hearts, write his law in the springs of their actions, so that obedience became a natural thing for them. Then would come complete restoration and the blotting out of all sin:

> I will make a new covenant with the house of Israel and the house of Judah, not like the covenant which I made with their fathers when I took them by the hand to bring them out of the land of Egypt, my covenant which they broke, though I was their husband, says the Lord.
>
> But this is the covenant which I will make with the house of Israel after those days, says the Lord: I will put my law within them, and I will write it upon their hearts; and I will be their God, and they shall be my people. And no longer shall each man teach his neighbour and each his brother, saying, Know the Lord, for they shall all know me, from the least of them to the greatest, says the Lord; for I will forgive their iniquity, and I will remember their sin no more. [Jer 31:31–34]

This is the language which our Lord used to describe what he had come to do. For the disciples, or for any Jew, there would be little need for extensive explanation. They knew what the covenant was and what it signified: they knew it by heart and it was the central theme of their prayers and of their worship. There was no need to tell them that blood was the principle of life,

nor that sacrifice was the giving of utter obedience
to God—the giving back of the steadfast love he
poured out to them—the giving back of the life he
gave and maintained in them. Every sacrifice they
attended and offered expressed this, and they
longed to be able to perform it perfectly, completely, so that God could again look on his creation and see that it was good. So, on the night
when he was betrayed,

> He took bread, and when he had given thanks
> he broke it and gave it to them, saying, This is
> my body which is given for you. Do this in re-
> membrance of me. And likewise the cup after
> supper, saying, This cup which is poured out
> for you is the new covenant in my blood.
> [Lk 22:19–20]

The next day he showed that the love of God was
steadfast despite any test that lay within human
experience, and that it was active in his world. It
would be a mistake to think that this was the
moment of our Lord's sacrifice, it was only one
moment in the eternal sacrifice which had been
from before the world began and would continue
until after the end of time: the mutually poured
love which flows between the Father and the Son.
But this was the moment when it was most plainly
to be seen, and in the cross and resurrection can
be seen the same power of God, bringing life out
of death, as the Hebrews saw in their escape from
Egypt.

The new covenant takes us into that sacrifice,
into the life of love which is the heart of God, for

Jesus Christ, the Son of God, shares his life with us in the new covenant. Through him we receive the fullness of God's steadfast love, and through him we are able in turn to return it to him. It is what we are made for.

For all the promises of God find their affirmation in him. That is why we utter the response through him, to the glory of God. [2 Cor 1:20]

Index of
names and subjects

David, 8, 9, 124, 125, 139, 146–7, 153, 166–67, 168, 170

Dedication of the First-Born, rite of, 109–110

Deuteronomic Code, 141ff. 155

EGYPT, ix, 42, 50–1, 62, 68

Israelites in exile, 72–95 passim, 101, 129, 169

escape from, see exodus

Ephraim, 63, 64–5

Esau, 54–7, 59, 61, 65

Elohist, or 'E' tradition, 74, 97, 98, 99

Exodus, ix, 5, 20, 27, 50, 70, 106–7, 108, 110–16, 130, 139, 140, 143, 148–50, 152, 163, 165, 169–73, 174–5

Book of, 72

Ezekiel, 13–14, 129, 153, 155

FALSE gods and religions, 11, 111, 139, 143, 158–9, 161–2

GENESIS, Book of, 27–8, 47–8

God:

his power, 16, 25, 27ff., 38, 50, 52, 66–7, 84–85, 86, 93–4, 129–30, 131, 174

his purpose for Israel, 17, 25, 29, 50, 53, 70

his steadfast love, 28f., 90, 174, 177–8

present and active in Jewish history, 3, 4, 52, 66–7, 84, 152, 154, 172

see also Yahweh

HEBREWS, 18, 25–7, 52, **137–54**

chosen people of God, x, 4, 51f., 70, 116, 129

entry into Canaan, 8–9, 157–69

made into a nation, ix–x, 1, 126–7, 128

their faith, 46, 69–70

Hebron (southern sanctuary), 42, 168

history, Hebrew, 1ff., 4, 22, 27, 138, 140

chiefly oral, 2, 6 (see also oral tradition)

dominated by exodus, 5–6

Hittites, 34, 82, 83, 158

Holiness Code, 140ff., 155

Hosea, 10, 90

Noah, 30, 41
Northern people (kingdom of Israel), 8, 9, 10, 63, 139, 166–8

ORAL tradition, 2ff., 6–8, 22–3, 51–2

PALESTINE, 8, 31ff., 83–4, 137, 166
Passover, 96, **102–8**, 109, 111, 116, 117, 152, 162, 163–4
Pentateuch, 4, 15, 18
  chart showing development, 23
  known as 'The Law', 7
Pharaoh, 50, 62
  during Egyptian exile, 72ff., 84f., 93–4, 96–7, 101–2, 106, 109, 111–14
  identity, 169
plagues, 96, 97–8, 99–101
  death of the first-born, 106, 108, 109–10
Priestly Code, 141ff.
Priestly, or 'P', tradition, 27ff., 47–8, 98, 99, 102–3, 116, 151
Priests, and the priesthood, 7–8, 12ff., 80–1, 92–3
  and the law, 80–1, 132, 138

Priests—(cont.)
  people of Israel are 'a kingdom of', 121–2, 133–4, 135
psalms, 14, 169–73

RACHEL, 57ff., 61–2, 144
Rebekah, 53–7
redemption, Hebrew meaning of, 67–8, 110
Red Sea, crossing of, 79, 96, 113–15, 116
  properly known as 'Sea of Reeds', 113
'Ritual Decalogue', 140ff., 162ff.

SAINT Paul, 46, 55, 85, 94, 95, 126, 156
Saint Peter, 85, 88, 95
Sarah, 39, 43ff., 53
Saul, 20, 125, 168
Second Isaiah, 16f., 26f.
Shechem (Northern Sanctuary), 7, 164–5, 166, 168
Solomon, 9, 124, 167
Southern people (kingdom of Judah), 8, 9, 12, 51, 63, 139, 166–8

TEN Commandments, 132, 140ff., 145, 155
'Twelve Curses', 140ff., 145

Index of biblical references